ALL ABOUT
VEGETARIAN COOKING

ALL ABOUT
VEGETARIAN COOKING

IRMA S. ROMBAUER
MARION ROMBAUER BECKER
ETHAN BECKER

PHOTOGRAPHY BY TUCKER & HOSSLER

A Dorling Kindersley Book

Dorling DK Kindersley

LONDON, NEW YORK, SYDNEY, DELHI, PARIS, MUNICH AND JOHANNESBURG

First published in Great Britain in 2001 by
Dorling Kindersley Limited, 9 Henrietta Street, London WC2E 8PS

Published by arrangement with the original publisher,
Scribner, an imprint of Simon & Schuster, Inc.

WELDON OWEN INC.
Chief Executive Officer: John Owen
President: Terry Newell
Chief Operating Officer: Larry Partington
Vice President, International Sales: Stuart Laurence
Publisher: Roger Shaw
Creative Director: Gaye Allen
Associate Publisher: Val Cipollone
Art Director: Jamie Leighton
Production Director: Stephanie Sherman
Designer: Crystal Guertin
Consulting Editors: Judith Dunham, Norman Kolpas
Assistant Editor: Anna Mantzaris
Studio Manager: Brynn Breuner
Pre-press Coordinator: Mario Amador
Production Manager: Chris Hemesath
Food Stylist: Jeff Tucker Prop Stylist: Sara Slavin
Food Styling Assistants: Rebecca Broder, Angela Kearney
Step-by-Step Photographer: Chris Shorten
Step-by-Step Food Stylist: Kim Brent

Joy of Cooking All About series was designed
and produced by Weldon Owen Inc.,
814 Montgomery Street, San Francisco,
California 94133, USA

Set in Joanna MT and Gill Sans

Reproduced by Bright Arts Singapore
Text film output by Mick Hodson Associates
Printed in Singapore by Tien Wah Press (Pte.) Ltd.

A CIP catalogue record for this book is available from
The British Library

ISBN 0 7513 3535 5

NOTE: Use either metric or imperial measurements since
conversions are not exact equivalents.

see our complete
catalogue at
www.dk.com

Recipe shown on half-title page:
Barbecued Aubergine and Roast Red Pepper Panini, 42
Recipe shown on title page:
Tart Greens with Apples, Pecans and Buttermilk Honey Dressing, 29

CONTENTS

FOREWORD

"To live we must eat. To live in health, we must eat intelligently," wrote my Granny Rom and my mother in the 1962 edition of the Joy of Cooking. More and more people today, for reasons of nutrition, ethics or faith, choose to live in health by eating a vegetarian diet.

That is why an entire volume in the new All About series is devoted to vegetarian cooking. It offers tips for planning vegetarian meals, information on key ingredients, and recipes for basic beans and grains, stocks and sauces — everything you need whether you're cooking for a casual luncheon or a special-occasion feast.

You might notice that this collection of kitchen-tested recipes is adapted from the latest edition of the Joy of Cooking. Just as our family has done for generations, we have worked to make this version of Joy a little bit better than the last. As a result, you'll find that some notes, recipes and techniques have been changed to improve their clarity and usefulness. Since 1931, the Joy of Cooking has constantly evolved. And now, the All About series has taken Joy to a whole new stage, as you will see from the beautiful colour photographs of finished dishes and clearly illustrated instructions for preparing and serving them. Granny Rom and Mother would have been delighted.

I'm sure you'll find All About Vegetarian Cooking to be both a useful and an enduring companion in your kitchen.

Enjoy!

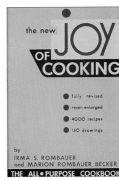

Ethan Becker pictured with his grandmother, Irma von Starkloff Rombauer (left), and his mother, Marion Rombauer Becker (right). Irma Rombauer published the first Joy of Cooking at her own expense in 1931. Marion Rombauer Becker became coauthor in 1951. Joy as it has progressed through the decades (from top left to bottom right): the 1931 edition with Marion's depiction of St. Martha of Bethany, said to be the patron saint of cooking, "slaying the dragon of kitchen drudgery"; the 1943 edition; the 1951 edition; the 1962 edition; the 1975 edition; and the 1997 edition.

About Vegetarian Cooking

So many people call themselves vegetarians these days that it's easy to fall into the mistaken belief that all vegetarians are alike. Such a simplistic point of view couldn't be further from the truth, and it gets in the way of understanding the many facets of vegetarian cooking and important related nutritional issues.

Vegetarians choose to be so for a wide variety of reasons. Many of the world's populations, such as the Hindus of India, follow vegetarian diets for religious reasons. Others follow near-vegetarian diets mandated by the scarcity of meat and other animal products in certain areas. Some people opt for a vegetarian diet as a consequence of ethical beliefs about animal rights. Growing numbers shun animal products for environmental reasons, claiming that growing plants is more ecologically efficient and responsible than raising livestock. Still others shift to a vegetarian diet to take advantage of the generally low-fat, cholesterol-free, high-fibre and nutrient-rich nature of plant foods.

Specific types of vegetarian diets vary as much as the reasons for choosing them. The major approaches are:

Lacto-vegetarian: Includes dairy products along with vegetables, fruits and grains, but eliminates eggs.

Ovo-vegetarian: Includes eggs along with vegetables, fruits and grains, but eliminates dairy products.

Lacto-ovo vegetarian: Includes dairy products and eggs along with vegetables, fruits and grains.

Macrobiotic: Emphasizes cooked foods, especially whole grains, with moderate amounts of vegetables and beans, minimal fruits, little if any dairy foods or eggs and occasional small servings of mild white fish.

Vegan: Rules out all animal products, including such staples as eggs and cheese, concentrating solely on vegetables, pulses, fruits and grains.

In addition, many people today may call themselves vegetarians while still including seafood in their diets. Or they may cut out only red meat, but eat both fish and poultry, or may indulge from time to time in poultry or meat, or even enjoy meals in which plant foods predominate but which may occasionally include very small amounts of animal protein. Such habits clearly push the envelope on the definition of "vegetarian". But vegetarians of all persuasions and preferences will find a bounty of useful and appealing recipes on the pages that follow. So, too, will those who want to add a greater variety of plant foods to their diets.

BUYING LOCALLY

Foods grown locally, most commonly found at farm shops and markets, do not require long-distance transportation and therefore do not contribute as greatly to pollution as items shipped long distances. Small-scale local farmers are also more adventurous in the variety of produce they grow, offering heirloom vegetables and fruits with dazzling colours, shapes, tastes and textures. They are also more likely to follow organic farming methods. Locally produced foods, organic or not, tend to be fresher and thus more flavourful and nutritious.

Organic Ingredients

Strong adherents to the philosophy that you are what you eat, many vegetarians seek out organic ingredients, and with good reason. Pesticides, insecticides, herbicides and fungicides are widely used in agriculture worldwide to protect food crops from worms, insects, weeds or fungi that may affect their quality and their profitability. Most of the produce we buy in the supermarket – virtually everything that isn't labelled "organic" – has been grown with one or more of these agents. Therefore, careful buying of ingredients and cleaning of produce are clearly important.

Whether or not you are a strict vegetarian, you should try, whenever possible, to buy organic products and other ingredients. Until recently, however, it has been difficult for consumers to be sure that the foods they are purchasing are indeed organic.

Although foods labelled organic are grown without the use of pesticides and their relatives, this does not guarantee that organic foods are 100 percent free of harmful chemicals, residuals of which may come from rainwater, irrigation water or the soil. Nor do tests show that organic foods are necessarily higher in nutrients or flavour. Buying such products, however, increases your odds of getting safer, better-quality, better-tasting ingredients than those that are mass-produced.

Just as important is supporting small-scale community-based farms. Agriculture is concentrated more and more in the hands of large corporations, and as a result, we are now able to buy almost any kind of "seasonal" food all year around, and often at very low prices. But there are hidden costs: the impact of the overuse of fertilizers and pesticides on the quality of our land, water and air; the despoiling of tropical forests and jungles to produce meat and winter vegetables; and the damage done to the birds, frogs, pollinating insects and other creatures with which we share our ecosystem. New methods of using and conserving land and water are badly needed.

We can look with some relief to the slow but steady increase in interest in organic farming methods; to the proliferation of Integrated Crop Management; to the increasing availability of organically grown produce, meat and milk; and to the success of cooks, bakers and food purveyors who use locally and organically produced ingredients skilfully, thus winning over more and more of the general population. Some guarded optimism might be appropriate. But to ensure that these trends continue, every one of us ought to take an active interest in the way our food is produced and processed. Pay attention to proposed legislative changes affecting food labelling, food safety, agricultural production, and the quality of our land, air and water, and let your legislators know how you feel about them. The political arena is full of lobbyists representing enterprises that would like to weaken regulations or shift the burden of compliance from industry to understaffed agencies. If we are what we eat, we need to do everything we can to protect our precious food resources.

Nutrition for Vegetarians

Most vegetarians follow healthful diets and as long as calories are adequate and food sources vary, vegetarian diets can provide all essential nutrients and are ample in protein. Vegetarian diets are also appropriate for children as long as they contain enough fats and calories and a sufficient variety of foods to support growth.

Achieving the goal of adequate calories and balanced and varied food sources may present a greater challenge to some vegetarians. Keep *Dietary Essentials*, 12, in mind when planning vegetarian diets. Also, pay close attention to the recommended daily servings on the Food Guide Pyramid (*below left*) and to the guidelines for serving sizes (*opposite*).

As indicated by the pyramid, food plants clearly constitute the foundation of a healthful diet, and therefore many servings of grains, vegetables and fruits should be chosen daily by vegetarians and nonvegetarians alike. Vegetarians who eliminate all meat, fish and poultry from their diets need to substitute other sources of protein, such as additional servings of beans and nuts.

The serving recommendations noted on the pyramid may seem unreasonable – who eats 6 to 11 servings of grain a day? But this is only because the Guide doesn't use the term *serving* the way most of us do. As the Guide defines the term,

FOOD GUIDE PYRAMID
Guide to Daily Food Choices

FATS, OILS, SWEETS — (Use sparingly)

(Up to 3 servings) — MILK, YOGHURT, CHEESE

MEAT, POULTRY, FISH, EGGS, BEANS, NUTS — (Up to 3 servings)

(3 to 5 servings) — VEGETABLES

FRUIT — (2 to 4 servings)

BREAD, CEREAL, RICE, PASTA — (6 to 11 servings)

At least 30 minutes of physical activity daily

Water as needed, usually six to eight 250ml glasses daily

Alcohol, optional for adults, in moderation (Up to 2 drinks per day for men, up to 1 drink per day for women)

THE VEGETARIAN DIET PYRAMID
Guide to Daily Food Choices

EGGS, SWEETS — Optional, or occasionally or in small quantities

EGG WHITES, SOY MILK, DAIRY

NUTS, SEEDS

PLANT OILS — Daily

WHOLE GRAINS

FRUITS, VEGETABLES

PULSES (SOY, BEANS, PEANUTS, OTHER PULSES) — At every meal

DAILY PHYSICAL ACTIVITY

Wine, beer and other alcohol (optional)

Drink enough water every day for good health

Copyright 1997 Oldways Preservation & Exchange Trust

a 2.5cm (1in) cube of cheese counts as a serving of dairy; a single serving of cold breakfast cereal (a grain) measures 30g (1oz); and an 185g (6oz) muffin from the bakery counts as 6 grain servings, the minimum recommendation for one day.

Not all nutritionists accept the Food Guide Pyramid as gospel. For example, proponents of the so-called Mediterranean diet – based originally on traditional consumption patterns in Greece and southern Italy, where heart disease and related ailments are comparatively rare – argue for a greater amount of fat, in the form of olive oil, cheese and yoghurt, than this Guide would prefer.

To show other healthful ways of eating, Oldways Preservation & Exchange Trust, a nonprofit educational organization based in Massachusetts, USA, has developed alternative pyramids. The one for vegetarians (*opposite right*) was created jointly by Oldways and the Harvard School of Public Health. Among its differences from the Food Guide pyramid, it places greater emphasis on the importance of all forms of pulses, singles out soy milk as an important part of the dairy group, and recommends less frequent consumption of whole eggs. At the foundation of the

vegetarian pyramid, and integral to it, is daily physical activity.

Most of us, though, do not always eat according to pyramids, charts and government regulations. We don't want to take all the fun out of eating, and indeed we shouldn't. What's important for following a vegetarian diet is to develop sensible eating habits overall, skewing our diet in the right direction. If we eat foods that are chosen according to sensible guidelines and are consumed in sensible amounts, all of the nutritional requirements will be met.

RULES FOR SERVING SIZES*

Protein Group (dried beans, eggs and nuts)
- 185-280g (6-9oz) cooked dried beans
- 2-3 eggs
- 2 tbsp peanut butter or 45g (1½ oz) nuts counts as ⅓ to ½ serving

Milk Group (milk, yoghurt and cheese)
- 250ml (8floz) milk or yoghurt
- 45g (1½ oz) natural cheese
- 60g (2oz) processed cheese

Grain Products Group (bread, cereal, rice and pasta)
- 1 slice bread
- 30g (1oz) ready-to-eat cereal
- 125g (4oz) cooked cereal, rice or pasta

Vegetable Group
- 125g (4oz) raw leafy vegetables
- 60g (2oz) other vegetables – cooked or raw
- 180ml (6floz) vegetable juice

Fruit Group
- 1 medium apple, banana or orange
- 90g (3oz) chopped, cooked or tinned fruit
- 180ml (6floz) fruit juice

Alcohol
- 375ml (12floz) beer or lager
- 160ml (5floz) wine
- 40ml (1½ floz) 80-proof distilled spirits

* Some foods fit into more than one group. Dried beans, peas and lentils are "crossover foods" that can be counted as servings in either the protein group or the vegetable group, but not both. Serving sizes indicated here are those used in the Food Guide Pyramid (*opposite left*) and are based on both suggested and usually consumed portions necessary to achieve adequate nutrient intake. They differ from serving sizes on the Nutrition Facts labels of packaged foods, which reflect portions usually consumed.

(Adapted from *The 1995 Dietary Guidelines for Americans,* 4th edition. USDA, USDHHS, HG 232)

Dietary Essentials

Although a varied vegetarian diet should provide all the nutrients you need, it is important to keep a few key nutrients in mind when planning meals.

Protein: Protein is essential for its nitrogen and amino acids, which are the building blocks for muscles, skin, connective tissues and almost every other body part. The chief components of protein are twenty amino acids that are needed to build tissue properly. Of these twenty, eleven are "nonessential", as your body is able to synthesize them on its own; the remaining nine cannot be synthesized and must be ingested regularly. These nine are known as essential amino acids. Protein from vegetable sources such as whole grains, nuts, seeds and pulses can satisfy all of your protein needs without meat consumption. However, because any given vegetable source will not provide all essential amino acids, it is important, especially for vegans, to eat a good variety of protein-rich vegetarian foods. Despite a commonly held belief, it is not necessary to combine different sources in the same meal to provide your body with complete proteins.

Iron: Your body needs iron to help build red blood cells and transport oxygen through the bloodstream. The most readily absorbable type of iron is present in animal proteins. Dairy products, eggs and plant foods, by contrast, contain iron of which only 2 to 20 percent is absorbable. That makes it all the more important for vegetarians to consume iron-rich foods such as leafy greens, whole grains, soybeans and tofu, members of the cabbage family and root vegetables. Eating foods rich in vitamin C, such as citrus fruits, blackcurrants, guavas, berries, broccoli and peppers, will also help increase iron absorption.

Vitamin B_{12}: Found only in animal products, this vitamin is essential for maintaining the nervous system and producing red blood cells. Vegetarians who eat dairy products should obtain sufficient quantities. Vegans, however, should take B_{12} supplements.

Vitamin D: Necessary for your body's absorption of calcium, the formation of teeth and bones and the functioning of the nervous system and muscles, this vitamin is synthesized by exposure to adequate sunlight. It is also present in commercially sold fortified milk. Particularly during winter months, vegans should take vitamin D supplements.

Energy intake: Very high-fibre diets, more likely to occur for vegetarians than nonvegetarians, can restrict somewhat the body's absorption of nutrients and intake of energy. Vegetarian parents should take special care that their children are getting sufficient nutrients and calories for proper development. So, too, should older people and pregnant or lactating women.

Planning Vegetarian Menus

Creating menus for your family and guests may seem challenging if you're new to following a vegetarian diet, but after a while, you'll find the process easy and enjoyable. Begin your planning by considering the season, for you will want to use, if possible, produce at its seasonal peak. Also take into account the climate, the time of day, the likes and dislikes of those at the table and, of course, your nutritional needs.

The following menus are examples of the many meals you can put together using the recipes in this book, substituting dishes to suit your tastes, talents and time. Countless other combinations can be devised. For a simple lunch or dinner, pair a salad made with fresh greens with a robust vegetable stew or pasta, or offer a hearty main-dish salad on its own. You'll find dishes made with grains, beans and tofu and plenty of vegetable dishes that can be served with them. Just add your favourite beverage and fresh fruit or other dessert to complete the meal.

MIDDLE EASTERN COCKTAIL PARTY
Hummus, 45
Baba Ghanoush, 45
Courgette Pancakes with Mint and
    Feta Cheese, 63
Greek Spinach and Cheese Pie, 69

ITALIAN GARDEN LUNCH
Rocket with Summer Vegetables, 28
Barbecued Pizza with Tomato and
    Three Cheeses, 48

FAMILY-STYLE SUPPER
Salad with Basic Vinaigrette, 27
Mushroom Ragout, 67
Oven-Baked Polenta, 108

ORIENTAL FEAST
Vegetarian Wonton Soup, 22
Stir-Fried Bok Choy with
    Mushrooms, 57
Szechuan Spiced Tofu, 87
Fried Rice, 101

SOUP AND SALAD
Deluxe Squash Soup, 21
Tart Greens with Apples, Pecans and
    Buttermilk Honey Dressing, 29

CASUAL INDIAN BUFFET
Potato and Aubergine Curry with
    Tomato and Fresh Coriander, 64
Saag Paneer, 64
Curried Chickpeas with
    Vegetables, 84
Basic Pilaf, 103

WARMING WINTER SUPPER
Winter Vegetable Couscous, 112
Harissa, 112

HEARTY BRUNCH
Huevos Rancheros, 119
Refried Beans, 81
Jícama Salad, 32

WEEKNIGHT SUPPER
Smoked Tofu Burgers, 87
Peruvian Potato Salad, 34
Rye Berry Salad with Roast Pepper
    Dressing, 37

MAKE-AHEAD LUNCH
Artichoke Frittata, 118
Chickpea Salad, 38
Focaccia, 42

ABOUT **STOCKS** & SOUPS

*I*f any food seems inherently calming, and even consoling, it is soup. Soup feels good when the weather gets cold. It restores our spirit and our vigour. (The first "restaurants" were eighteenth-century Parisian establishments that served rich soups to restore, or restaurer, the hungry citizenry.) In the old days, when a "soup batch" of vegetables and herbs cost a few pence, home cooks routinely made soups from scratch. Today, the smell of soup simmering still symbolizes home cooking.

Soup of Garden Greens with Parmesan Threads, 19

Preparing Stocks

Stocks are a vital ingredient in many sauces, soups and other foods, and no shop-bought variety can compare with a well-tended homemade version. Stock making is different from other kinds of cooking. Instead of calling for tender, young ingredients, stocks are best made with mature vegetables, cooked slowly for a long time to extract every vestige of flavour.

The characteristics of any good stock are flavour, body and clarity. Of the three, flavour is paramount, and the way to get it is by using a high proportion of ingredients to water. The most flavourful stocks are made with only enough water to cover the vegetables. Additional water is needed only when the liquid evaporates below the level of the ingredients before the stock is fully cooked. Follow the stock recipes for ideal ratios of liquid to solids, but the principle is simple: keep the solids covered while cooking.

Vegetable stocks rarely require more than an hour to cook. In fact, their delicate flavours deteriorate if overcooked. When preparing ingredients for stock making, it is important to chop vegetables to size according to their cooking times – large for long cooking and small for quick cooking – to allow their flavours to be fully extracted.

HOW TO STRAIN AND STORE STOCK

It is easy to strain and store your own stock at home. When the stock is chilled, any fat will rise in a solid mass that must be removed before reheating. While cold, this fat layer actually protects the stock.

1 When the stock has finished cooking, strain it through a fine-mesh sieve (or a colander lined with a double layer of muslin or a coffee filter) into another pot or a large heatproof container and discard the solids. We recommend pressing heavily on the solids while straining for the vegetable stock recipes, where the extra flavour from the cooked vegetables is needed. Do not let the stock sit out at room temperature for long as it is a good breeding ground for bacteria.

2 Speed up the cooling process by placing the hot pot, uncovered, in a sink or bowl of iced water and stirring it a few times. Once the stock cools enough so that it will not raise the temperature of your refrigerator, cover it tightly and chill it.

3 Stock will keep for 3 to 5 days in the refrigerator. If refrigerated for longer, boil the stock for 10 minutes, then refrigerate it for another 3 to 5 days. For prolonged storage, transfer stock to pint or litre plastic containers or plastic freezer bags and freeze it. Small amounts of stock can also be frozen in ice cube trays.

Vegetable Stock

About 1 litre (1½ pints)

Beyond the standard recipe here, vegetable stocks allow for much improvisation. Good additions include potatoes, corncobs, fennel, ginger, washed organic vegetable skins and even a few tablespoons of lentils. A small amount of soy sauce and a pinch of crushed chilli flakes can also be added. Vegetables to avoid include those in the cabbage family (except when used deliberately and with discretion), aubergine and most strong greens (with the exception of kale); too many carrots or parsnips will turn the stock overly sweet (we like to include a small turnip to add complexity to the stock and to offset the sweetness of the carrot). When possible, tailor the ingredients to suit the recipe the stock will be used in. For example, a stock accented with ginger and garlic would be good in many Oriental recipes. In general, 750g (1¼ lb)

vegetables to 1.5 litres (2½ pints) water makes about 750ml to 1 litre (1¼ to 1½ pints) stock.

Combine in a stockpot:

1 medium onion, sliced
1 leek, white part only, cleaned thoroughly and sliced
1 carrot, peeled and sliced
1 small turnip, peeled and sliced
6 cloves garlic, peeled and smashed
1.5 litres (2½ pints) cold water
1 *Bouquet Garni*, right

Simmer gently, partially covered, until the vegetables are completely softened, 45 to 60 minutes. Strain into a clean pot or heatproof plastic container, pressing down on the vegetables to extract the juices. Season with:

Salt and ground black pepper

Let cool, uncovered, then refrigerate until ready to use.

Bouquet Garni

Since herbs tend to float, we recommend tying them together in a little packet, known as a bouquet garni. Vary the contents to suit your dish, with additions such as whole cloves, dill, lemon zest or garlic. For express broth or quick-cooking stocks, there is no need to tie the seasonings in a bundle – they can simply be tossed in with the vegetables.

Wrap in a 10 ×10cm (4 × 4in) piece of muslin:

Small bunch of parsley or parsley stems
8 sprigs fresh thyme, or 1 tsp dried
1 bay leaf
2 or 3 celery leaves (optional)

Tie the muslin securely with a piece of kitchen string or omit the muslin and simply tie the herbs together at their stems. Refrigerate in a tightly covered container until ready to use.

Roast Vegetable Stock

About 1 litre (1¼ pints)

Preheat the oven to 200°C (400°F) Gas 6. Lightly grease a roasting tin. Toss together in the prepared tin and roast, stirring occasionally, until well browned, about 1 hour:

250g (8oz) mushrooms or mushroom stems, wiped clean
1 onion, quartered
2 carrots, peeled and cut into 5cm (2in) pieces
8 cloves garlic, peeled and smashed
1 small turnip, peeled and cut into 5cm (2in) pieces

Remove the vegetables to a stockpot, then deglaze the hot roasting tin by adding:

250ml (8floz) cold water

Scrape up any browned bits, then add the liquid to the pot along with:

1.5 litres (2½ pints) cold water
1 *Bouquet Garni*, right, including a pinch of crushed chilli flakes

Simmer gently, uncovered, until the vegetables are completely softened, 45 to 60 minutes. Strain into a clean pot or heatproof plastic container, pressing down on the vegetables to extract the juices. Season with:

Salt to taste

Let cool, uncovered, then refrigerate until ready to use.

Cajun Black-Eyed Bean Soup

About 2 litres (3¼ pints)

The Louisiana culinary trinity – onions, peppers, and celery – flavours this hearty country soup.

Rinse, sort and soak, 78:

500g (1lb) dried black-eyed beans

In a soup pot, gently cook, covered, but stirring occasionally, until tender, but not brown:

3 medium stalks celery, diced
2 medium onions, diced
1 medium green pepper, diced
1 medium red pepper, diced
2 cloves garlic, finely chopped
3 tbsp vegetable oil

Drain and add the black-eyed beans along with:

2.5 litres (4 pints) cold water

Simmer, partially covered, until the beans are tender, about 1 hour. Using a potato masher, mash just enough beans in the pot to slightly thicken the soup. Season with:

2 tbsp Worcestershire sauce
2-3 tsp Tabasco sauce, or to taste
1 tbsp salt

Ladle into warmed bowls. Garnish with:

Sliced spring onion greens

BLACK-EYED BEANS

Black-eyed beans are members of the mung bean family. They have a fuller vegetable flavour than most beans. A small black dot, which remains visible after cooking, names the cream-coloured beans, which are known in the US as black-eyed peas or black-eye Susans. If you wish to substitute fresh or frozen black-eyed beans for dried, use three times the amount called for and cook just until the beans are tender, 15 to 30 minutes, depending on the maturity and whether they are frozen.

Broccoli Cheddar Soup

About 1.5 litres (2½ pints)

This is a good soup to add to your permanent repertoire. It can be made quickly with ingredients often at hand, and it solves the problem of what to make for dinner when accompanied by a big salad and a loaf of good bread.

In a soup pot, melt over medium-low heat:

45g (1½ oz) unsalted butter or 3 tbsp vegetable oil

Add:

125g (4oz) chopped onions, or leeks, cleaned thoroughly
90g (3oz) chopped celery
375g (12oz) broccoli florets, coarsely chopped

Cook, stirring, until tender, about 5 minutes. Sprinkle over the top:

60g (2oz) plain flour

Stir well to blend, increase the heat to medium and cook, stirring constantly, for 5 minutes. (Make sure not to burn the flour.) Gradually add and stir until smooth:

1 litre (1½ pints) *Vegetable Stock, 17*
500ml (16floz) milk

Cook until the vegetables are tender, about 5 minutes more. Transfer to a food processor and purée until smooth. Return the soup to the pot and return to a low simmer. Stir in in batches, blending well after each addition:

185g (6oz) grated Cheddar cheese

Be very careful not to boil this soup: If the soup is too hot the cheese will break down. Season with:

1 tbsp Dijon mustard
¼ tsp ground black pepper
Salt to taste
Tabasco sauce to taste (optional)
Worcestershire sauce to taste (optional)

Garnish the soup with:

Grated Cheddar cheese

Soup of Garden Greens with Parmesan Threads

About 2.5 litres (4 pints)

Fresh herbs bring vibrance, while a good Parmesan cheese lends an appealing nuttiness to this quick vegetable soup. Add and subtract vegetables depending on what the garden and market yield. Serve with a whole-grain bread.

In a large soup pot, cook, stirring, over medium-low heat until wilted, about 10 minutes:

2 medium carrots, peeled and finely diced
2 medium courgettes, finely diced
2 large onions, finely diced

in:

2 tbsp extra-virgin olive oil

Add:

2-2.5 litres (3¼-4 pints) *Vegetable Stock, 17*

If not using fresh herbs at the end, add:

2 tsp dried basil
½ tsp dried oregano

Boil, partially covered, until the vegetables are tender, about 10 minutes. Meanwhile beat together and set aside:

2 large eggs
90g (3oz) freshly grated Parmesan

Drop into the soup and simmer, uncovered, 1 minute:

6 large cos or escarole leaves, shredded
5 tbsp chopped fresh basil
5 tbsp chopped fresh parsley
1 tbsp chopped fresh oregano

Remove the soup from the heat and whisk in the egg mixture, stirring slowly so that it forms thin, firm threads. Season to taste with:

Salt and ground black pepper

Serve hot.

PARMIGIANO-REGGIANO

This mouth-filling cow's milk cheese with a complex and pleasing aftertaste is made in a small, legally designated area of Emilia-Romagna in northern Italy. It is the only true Parmesan. All the others are imitations. Remember that older is not better. Today's Parmigiano-Reggiano usually reaches its peak at about two years. Before World War II, when different cows gave Parmigiano-Reggiano milk, the cheese successfully aged longer. Grana Padano is equally good on pasta, or alternatively you can substitute a good, mature Cheddar. Grated Parmigiano-Reggiano is a wonderful addition to soups. This cheese is also excellent simply picked up in the fingers and nibbled after informal Italian meals.

Spinach Soup

About 1.25 litres (2 pints)

In a soup pot, cook, stirring, over medium-low heat until tender but not brown:

4 tbsp finely chopped onion
2 cloves garlic, finely chopped
in:
30g (1oz) unsalted butter
Stir in:
2 tbsp plain flour
Cook, stirring constantly, over medium heat for 5 minutes. Do not brown the flour. Gradually whisk in:
1 litre (1½ pints) milk
Simmer, stirring occasionally, over low heat, until slightly thickened, about 10 minutes. Meanwhile bring a large pot of water to a boil. Stem and wash thoroughly:
500g (1lb) spinach
Plunge the spinach leaves in the boiling water for 1 minute. Immediately drain and rinse with cold water. Purée until smooth. Add half the soup to the spinach and continue to process until smooth. Stir the purée into the remaining soup (*opposite*).
Season with:
1 tsp salt
¼ tsp freshly grated or ground nutmeg
¼ tsp ground black pepper

Escarole, Garlic and Tomato Soup

About 1.25 litres (2 pints)

In a soup pot, cook, stirring, over medium-low heat, until tender but not brown:

1 medium onion, chopped
5 cloves garlic, finely chopped
in:
3 tbsp olive oil or other vegetable oil
Add:
2 medium, ripe tomatoes, peeled, seeded, chopped, with their juices reserved
750ml (24floz) *Vegetable Stock*, 17
Bring to a boil. Reduce the heat and simmer, uncovered, 5 minutes. Add:
1 small head escarole, coarsely chopped
1 tsp salt
¼ to ½ tsp ground black pepper
Simmer, uncovered, until the escarole is softened, about 5 minutes. Ladle into warmed bowls. Garnish with:
Chopped fresh basil or *Pesto Sauce*, 96 (optional)

Deluxe Squash Soup

About 1.5 litres (2½ pints)

Preheat the oven to 200°C (400°F) Gas 6. Place on a large baking sheet:
1 large butternut squash
Drizzle over the top:
2 tbsp olive oil
Roast for 45 minutes. Cover the squash with foil and roast until tender, about 15 more minutes. When cool enough to handle, scrape the pulp from the skin into a food processor and pour in the pan juices. Add and purée until smooth:
250ml (8floz) *Vegetable Stock*, 17
In a large saucepan, heat over medium-low heat:
2 tbsp olive oil
Add and cook, stirring, until tender but not brown, about 5 minutes:
1 small onion, finely chopped
1 small carrot, finely chopped
1 stalk celery, finely chopped
Add the puréed squash along with:
¼ tsp ground cinnamon
¼ tsp ground nutmeg
¼ tsp ground ginger
Add:
1 litre (1½ pints) *Vegetable Stock*, 17
Bring to a boil, reduce the heat to medium and simmer, stirring from time to time, until the vegetables are tender, about 10 minutes. Stir in:
125ml (4floz) double cream
Season to taste with:
Salt and ground black pepper
Divide among 6 soup bowls:
250g (8oz) cooked wild rice
Ladle the soup over the rice and serve.

Vegetarian Wonton Soup

6 to 8 servings; 1.5 litres (2½ pints) soup and about 30 wontons

Homemade wontons are easy to prepare with readily available premade wrappers. When cooking wontons, keep the water at a low simmer to prevent them from opening. Fresh or dried mushrooms can be used in this filling.
Either soak for 30 minutes:

**6 dried medium shiitake
   mushrooms (optional)**
in:

500ml (16floz) hot water
Drain the mushrooms, straining the soaking liquid through a fine-mesh sieve lined with a dampened paper towel. Remove the mushroom stems, and thinly slice.
Or thinly slice:

8 fresh shiitake mushrooms
In a large frying pan, heat over medium heat:

1 tbsp vegetable oil
Add the shiitake mushrooms along with:

**155g (5oz) chopped white
   mushrooms**
**250g (8oz) firm tofu, drained and
   crumbled**
2 spring onions, chopped

**45g (1½ oz) thinly sliced Chinese
   cabbage**
1 tbsp chopped fresh ginger
Sauté until the vegetables are wilted, about 5 minutes.
Let cool, then season with:

2 tbsp light or dark soy sauce
1 tbsp toasted sesame oil
1 tbsp dry sherry or Shaoxing wine
1 tsp chilli oil (optional)
1 tsp sugar
½ tsp salt
⅛ tsp ground black pepper
In a small bowl, stir together:

1 large egg
1 tbsp water
Working in batches of 10 at a time, lay out the first batch of:

Wonton wrappers
To assemble, arrange wrappers so that one point is facing you, in a diamond pattern. Lightly brush each wrapper with the egg wash. Place a teaspoonful of filling in the centre of each wrapper. Fold the wonton in half, by bringing the top corner to meet the bottom corner, forming a triangle. Seal by pressing

the edges firmly, squeezing all the air out as you seal. To finish, bring the two outside corners to meet at the centre and press to seal. If the wonton wrappers start to dry out, moisten the corners with egg wash. When all the wontons are assembled, set aside.
In a soup pot, bring to a simmer:

**1.25 litres (2 pints) *Vegetable Stock*, 17,
   or 250ml (8floz) reserved
   mushroom-soaking liquid and
   1 litre (1½ pints) *Vegetable Stock***
Season with:

1⅛ tsp salt
Cover and keep warm.
Bring a large pot of water to a simmer. Drop in the wontons in 2 or 3 batches and simmer gently until done, about 5 minutes. Drain, then divide among individual bowls. Ladle the hot broth over the wontons.
Garnish with:

Decoratively cut carrots
Chopped spring onion greens

ABOUT
SALADS

Although the term salad once meant nothing more than lettuce tossed with oil and vinegar, today's salads are made from almost every sort of vegetable, pasta, grain or pulse, raw or cooked, cold or warm, tied together by a flavourful dressing. Every step in creating a salad, from selecting ingredients to serving it, allows for the cook's imagination to play its part.

A simple green salad is an excellent way to refresh the palate after the main course of a large dinner and a perfect preparation for the dessert to come. A plate of marinated vegetables will spark the appetite before the main course. Salads can also replace vegetable side dishes. And finally, there are more and more instances where salad becomes the entire meal.

Tart Greens with Apples, Pecans and Buttermilk Honey Dressing, 29

Preparing Greens for Salads

Buy the freshest greens with crisp leaves, free of brown spots on leaves or stems. Greens still attached to their roots are usually more intense in flavour than those severed at the stem. Use greens as soon as possible after buying them. If you have to store them, remove any leaves that are wilted or show signs of decay and take off any rubber or metal bands holding greens together. Unwashed greens will keep for 3 to 4 days at most. Store greens in the vegetable bin of your refrigerator in a plastic bag with holes poked in it. Properly washing, drying and chilling salad greens is the indispensable first step in any salad.

Always handle greens carefully, so as not to bruise them. The easiest way to wash them is to separate the leaves and place them in a large bowl or sink full of cold water, swish them around for 30 seconds

or so, then lift them from the water gently so that the dirt and grit remain in the water. Repeat the process until the water is clear.

For drying, salad spinners are a wonderful convenience. Over-crowding a salad spinner, however, will both bruise the greens and hinder the device's ability to dry them adequately. A spinner about one-half to two-thirds full will work perfectly every time. Alternatively, dry greens by tossing lightly in a colander, tapping your fingers against the underside of the colander to make sure all the water runs out. In either case, it will probably be necessary to wrap them in absorbent paper towels for the final drying. Whatever the method, once dried, the greens should be well chilled to render them crisp. Tear or cut them only when you are about to make the salad.

Garnishing Green Salads

A green salad is easily transformed into a main course with the addition of a few ingredients chosen for texture, taste and visual appeal. The greens remain dominant in these salads, so avoid the temptation to overwhelm them with too many bits of this and that. Think in terms of balance and harmony. Too many assertive garnishes will cancel each other out. On the other hand, too many sweet flavours – fruit, soft cheese, carrots and tomatoes – may become cloying. Begin by tasting the greens. If they are strong and pun-gent, they can support more flavour;

mild and tender greens tolerate less. The simplest way to enhance a green salad is to add condiments or seasonings to the salad while or after you toss it with the dressing. Be sure to give the greens a few extra tosses to integrate the additions well. With a light coat of dressing on the greens, small accents such as croutons, nuts, cheese and olives will cling to the salad and are less apt to fall to the bottom of the bowl. For more substantial additions like the multiple ingredients of a Greek salad, everything gets tossed together at once.

Dressing Salads

The time to dress green salads is always at the very last minute. Once dressed, greens become limp if they sit too long. Place the greens in a bowl large enough to hold them spaciously. Pour the dressing or its ingredients down the side to form a puddle at the bottom. The tossing can now be done with clean hands, a pair of tongs, a couple of ordinary wooden kitchen spoons or the oversized fork and spoon known as salad servers. Reach into the bottom of the bowl and gently lift the greens so that the topmost greens fall to the bottom. Gently repeat this action until all the dressing is distributed.

MAKING A VINAIGRETTE

The most surefire way to make a thick, well-emulsified vinaigrette is to first whisk together the vinegar or lemon juice and the seasonings (salt, chopped shallots or other members of the onion tribe and mustard) in a small bowl. Then slowly add the oil, drop by drop, whisking as you go, until the dressing begins to thicken. Add the oil in more of a steady stream as the dressing becomes noticeably thicker.

An alternative, and perhaps more convenient, technique is to place the vinegar or lemon juice and seasonings in a small jar with a tight-fitting lid and shake to blend. Then add the oil in three or four additions, shaking vigorously between additions. A third and equally popular method is to mix the vinegar and seasonings in a blender and then add the oil in a slow, steady stream with the machine running. Vinaigrette can be stored, tightly covered, in the refrigerator for up to 2 weeks. Always whisk dressings briskly just before adding them to salads so that the ingredients are well mixed and in balance, and don't add more vinaigrette than is necessary to lightly coat the salad.

Basic Vinaigrette

About 375ml (12floz)

The optional ingredients help maintain the emulsion of oil and vinegar.
If garlic flavour is desired, mash together until a paste is formed:
1 small clove garlic, peeled
2 to 3 pinches of salt
Remove to a small bowl or a jar with a tight-fitting lid. Add and whisk or shake until well blended:
80-125ml (3-4floz) red wine vinegar or fresh lemon juice
1 shallot, chopped
1 tsp Dijon mustard (optional)
Salt and ground black pepper to taste
Add in a slow, steady stream, whisking constantly, or add to the jar and shake until smooth:
250ml (8floz) extra-virgin olive oil
Taste and adjust the seasonings. Use at once or cover and refrigerate.

FRESH HERB VINAIGRETTE

Prepare *Basic Vinaigrette, left,* adding 5 tbsp chopped or snipped fresh herbs (basil, dill, parsley, chives and/or thyme).

LEMON CAPER VINAIGRETTE

Prepare *Basic Vinaigrette, left,* with fresh lemon juice and add 1 tbsp chopped drained capers, 1 tbsp chopped fresh parsley, and ½ tsp finely grated lemon zest.

BASIL CHIVE VINAIGRETTE

Prepare *Basic Vinaigrette, left,* adding 5 tbsp chopped fresh basil, 5 tbsp finely snipped fresh chives, and, if desired, 1 tbsp walnut oil.

GREEN PEPPERCORN VINAIGRETTE

Prepare *Basic Vinaigrette, left,* adding 2 tbsp finely chopped drained green peppercorns or 1 tbsp cracked dried green peppercorns.

LIME VINAIGRETTE

Prepare *Basic Vinaigrette, left,* substituting 60ml (2floz) fresh lime juice for the vinegar or lemon juice and, if desired, adding a large pinch of toasted cumin seeds.

BLACK PEPPER VINAIGRETTE

Prepare *Basic Vinaigrette, left,* adding 1 tsp finely grated lemon zest and 2 tsp cracked black peppercorns, or to taste.

Rocket with Summer Vegetables

4 to 6 servings

Use this recipe as a rough guideline, substituting whatever summer vegetables are most plentiful in the market. Baby turnip or beetroot greens or Swiss chard leaves can be substituted for the rocket.

Prepare:

Basic Vinaigrette, 27, or one of the variations

Cook in a large pot of boiling water for about 1 minute:

1 small courgette, cut into 1cm (½ in) cubes, or 6 pattypan squash, cut in half

Remove with a large slotted spoon, refresh in ice water, and drain well. Add to the boiling water:

250g (8oz) thin green beans, trimmed

Cook just until crisp-tender, about 1 minute. Remove with a large slotted spoon, refresh in iced water, and drain well. Combine the squash and green beans in a salad bowl along with:

315g (10oz) cherry tomatoes, halved

1 small red onion, halved and very thinly sliced

5 tbsp chopped fresh basil

Toss well with enough of the vinaigrette to coat. Taste and adjust the seasonings. Divide among salad plates:

250g (8oz) bite-sized pieces rocket and cos lettuce, washed and dried

Spoon the vegetables on top. Drizzle more dressing over the salads and garnish with:

Fresh basil leaves (optional)

Serve immediately.

Tart Greens with Apples, Pecans and Buttermilk Honey Dressing

4 to 6 servings

Whisk together in a small bowl:
60ml (2floz) cider vinegar
60ml (2floz) sour cream
60ml (2floz) buttermilk
3 tbsp honey
1 tsp finely chopped garlic
1 spring onion, finely chopped
Pinch of cayenne pepper
Salt and ground black pepper to taste
Add in a slow, steady stream,

whisking constantly:
125ml (4floz) olive oil
Combine in a salad bowl:
185g (6oz) bite-sized pieces rocket, washed and dried
1 small head radicchio, washed, dried and torn into bite-sized pieces
2 heads chicory, washed, dried and sliced lengthwise into long strips

Stir the dressing well, add just enough to moisten the greens, and toss to coat. Divide the greens among salad plates and top with:
2 Granny Smith or other tart apples, cored and very thinly sliced
60g (2oz) pecan halves, toasted
Serve immediately.

Tomato and Mozzarella Salad (Insalata Caprese)

4 to 6 servings

Named for the island of Capri, where it was perhaps first made, this gloriously simple salad is popular all over Italy and is increasingly so in this country. Be sure to use the ripest tomatoes, the freshest mozzarella and the best extra-virgin olive oil you can find.

Arrange, alternating the tomato and mozzarella slices, on a platter:
4 large ripe tomatoes, cut into 1cm (½in) thick slices
375g (12oz) mozzarella cheese, cut into 5mm (¼in) thick slices
Sprinkle with:
45g (1½oz) fresh basil leaves

Drizzle over the salad:
125ml (4floz) olive oil, preferably extra-virgin
Salt to taste
Serve at once or let stand at room temperature for up to 1 hour before serving. In either case, do not refrigerate the salad.

Baked Goat's Cheese and Baby Greens

4 servings

Mesclun includes many different salad greens and herbs, each varying in flavour, texture and colour. A mix might contain red- and green-tipped oakleaf lettuce, rocket, cos lettuce, chervil, colourful red radicchio, curly white as well as green frisée, escarole and bitter dandelion greens. Add fresh herbs to this mixture (sage, dill and tarragon are our favourites), top with baked goat's cheese, serve with some toasted bread and you have a delicious lunch or supper dish.

Preheat the oven to 200°C (400°F) Gas 6. Grease a small baking dish.
Refrigerate in a salad bowl:
375g (12oz) mixed baby greens or mesclun, washed and dried
Stir together in a shallow bowl:
90g (3oz) fine dry breadcrumbs
1 tsp dried thyme
Pour into another shallow bowl:
60ml (2floz) extra-virgin olive oil
Coat first with the olive oil and then with the breadcrumbs:
4 rounds fresh goat's cheese, each

about 6cm (2½in) in diameter and 1cm (½in) thick
Place the cheese in the baking dish and bake until golden brown and lightly bubbling, about 6 minutes. Meanwhile, prepare:
Basic Vinaigrette, 27
Toss the greens with just enough vinaigrette to coat and divide among 4 salad plates. Place a round of baked cheese in the centre of each salad and serve at once.

Barbecued Ratatouille Salad

6 servings

Prepare a medium-hot charcoal fire. Combine in a bowl:

2-4 tbsp olive oil

2-3 tbsp red wine vinegar, to taste

When the coals are covered with grey ash, coat with the oil mixture:

Twelve aubergine slices, cut 1cm (½ in) thick

2 fennel bulbs, quartered lengthwise

2 medium courgettes, cut lengthwise into thick slices

4 plum tomatoes

3 slender leeks (white part only), split up to the root ends and washed thoroughly

3 red, orange or yellow peppers, or a combination

½ head garlic, unpeeled

Barbecue the vegetables, turning as needed, until the tomatoes and peppers are charred on the outside and the other vegetables are tender, about 5 minutes for the courgettes, up to 20 minutes for the garlic. Remove from the barbecue and let cool slightly. Peel, seed and dice the tomatoes and peppers. Dice the fennel and courgettes into 1cm (½ in) pieces. Trim the root ends from the leeks and slice. Squeeze the garlic cloves from their skins and mash. Combine the vegetables, except the aubergine slices, in a bowl. Just before serving, stir in:

3 tbsp chopped fresh basil

1 tbsp extra-virgin olive oil

Pinch of grated orange zest

Salt and ground black pepper to taste

Arrange the aubergine slices on a platter, top with the ratatouille and serve at room temperature.

Avocado and Mango Salad

4 servings

This salad is luscious with either mango or papaya – choose whichever you find is the ripest. The mango and the avocado are the centrepieces here, not the greens.

Halve:

1 lemon

Halve, peel and thinly slice lengthwise:

2 ripe avocados

Gently rub the slices with the lemon halves. Slice vertically into segments:

1 ripe mango or papaya, peeled

Combine in a small bowl:

1 large red onion, thinly sliced

125ml (4floz) fresh lemon juice

Pinch of salt

Whisk together in a small bowl:

125ml (4floz) olive oil

2 tbsp fresh lemon juice

Salt and ground black pepper to taste

Toss with half of the dressing:

125g (4oz) rocket leaves, washed and dried

Divide among chilled salad plates. Around the rocket, alternate slices of avocado and mango. Spoon the remaining dressing over the slices. Arrange the onion over the rocket. Serve immediately.

Cold Asparagus Salad with Sesame Seeds

4 to 6 servings

Asparagus spears poke through the earth in spring. If not picked, these young shoots grow into tall ferny branches with bright red berries. The thinner the shoot, the younger and, usually, the more tender. They can be green, purple or green and purple; cream-coloured shoots have been raised without sunlight. Select crisp, tightly closed stalks whose cut ends are not dry.

Whisk together in a small bowl:

3 tbsp toasted sesame oil
4 tsp white wine vinegar
4 tsp light or dark soy sauce
2½ tbsp sugar

Toast in a small frying pan until golden brown:

4 tsp sesame seeds

Immediately stir into the dressing. Place in a large pot of boiling water:

750g (1½ lb) asparagus, peeled and cut diagonally into 5cm (2in) pieces

Cook for no more than 1½ minutes for thin asparagus or 2½ minutes for thicker. Immediately drain and refill the pot with cold running water until all the heat has left the asparagus. Drain again and dry thoroughly. Cover and refrigerate until the salad is cold, about 1 hour. Toss with the dressing. Serve.

PEA SALAD

Prepare the dressing for *Cold Asparagus Salad with Sesame Seeds, left.* Cook 90g (3oz) sugar snap peas in a large saucepan of boiling salted water for 2 minutes. Add 45g (1½ oz) mange tout and 90g (3oz) fresh or thawed frozen petit pois and cook for 1 minute. Drain, rinse and drain again as for the asparagus. Pat dry. Toss the peas and dressing together in a bowl with 315g (10oz) pea shoots, washed and dried. Serve at once.

Pitta Salad (Fattoush)

4 servings

Toss together in a colander:

1 small cucumber, peeled, seeded and cut into 1cm (½ in) cubes

1 tsp salt

Let stand to drain for 30 minutes. Preheat the oven to 180°C (350°F) Gas 4.

On a baking tray, bake until crisp and lightly browned, about 10 minutes:

Two pitta breads, split open

Break into bite-sized pieces.

Press the excess water out of the cucumbers, rinse quickly, and blot dry. Combine the cucumbers in a medium bowl with:

3 medium, ripe tomatoes, chopped

1 small green pepper, diced

6 spring onions, white and tender green parts, finely chopped

5 tbsp chopped fresh parsley

2 tbsp chopped fresh coriander

1 tbsp finely chopped fresh mint

Whisk together in a small bowl:

80ml (3 floz) olive oil, preferably extra-virgin

Juice of 1 large lemon (about 60ml/2 floz)

1 clove garlic, crushed

¼ tsp salt

Pour the dressing over the vegetables and toss well. Add the pitta toasts, toss again and serve immediately.

Cucumber and Yoghurt Salad (Tzatziki)

4 to 6 servings

Set a very fine mesh sieve or a colander lined with several layers of muslin over a bowl. Add and let drain at room temperature for at least 2 hours or, covered, in the refrigerator for up to 24 hours:

500ml (16 floz) yoghurt

Toss together in a colander:

1 large cucumber, peeled, seeded and diced

1 tsp salt

Let stand to drain for 30 minutes. Press the excess water out of the cucumbers, rinse quickly, and blot dry. Mash together until a paste is formed:

2 cloves garlic, peeled

2-3 pinches of salt

Combine the yoghurt, cucumbers and garlic in a medium bowl along

with:

2-3 tsp white wine vinegar

2 tsp chopped fresh mint

2 tsp snipped fresh dill

Salt and ground white pepper to taste

Drizzle over the salad:

1 tbsp olive oil, preferably extra-virgin

Jícama Salad

8 servings

The lime and ground chilli peppers are the perfect complements to jícama's slightly sweet flavour.

Peel and halve lengthwise:

1 medium jícama, about 500g (1lb)

Lay each half on its cut side, slice 5mm (¼ in) thick, and cut the slices diagonally in half.

Cut diagonally into 5mm (¼ in) thick slices:

2 small cucumbers, halved lengthwise and seeded

Cut a slice off the stem and blossom ends of:

3 medium navel oranges

Stand the oranges on a chopping board and cut away the peel and all the white pith. Halve lengthwise, then cut crosswise into 5mm (¼ in) thick slices. In a large bowl, toss the jícama, cucumbers and oranges with:

6 radishes, thinly sliced

1 small red onion, thinly sliced

Juice of 2 limes, about 80ml (3 floz)

Let stand for 20 minutes, then season with:

Salt to taste

To serve, spoon the salad onto a platter and drizzle the accumulated juices on top. Sprinkle with:

About 2 tsp ground chilli pepper, preferably ancho or guajillo

About 5 tbsp coarsely chopped fresh coriander

Sicilian Salad

4 to 6 servings

This is an easy salad to make and is just as good when made without the fennel or olives.

Cut a slice off the stem and blossom ends of:

4 medium navel oranges

Stand the oranges on a chopping board and cut away the peel and all the white pith. On a plate cut cross-wise into 5mm (¼in) thick slices. Arrange the slices on a platter and pour the juice over them. Arrange with the orange slices:

1 small red onion, thinly sliced

3 small fennel bulbs, thinly sliced (optional)

90g (3oz) stoned black Gaeta olives (optional)

Sprinkle with:

6 fresh mint leaves, finely chopped

Ground black pepper to taste

Drizzle over the salad:

2 tbsp olive oil, or more to taste

Let stand for about 2 hours at room temperature before serving.

Peruvian Potato Salad

4 servings; about 330ml (11floz) sauce

This salad is most flavourful when the potatoes are warm, but it is equally enjoyable when chilled. Use Peruvian blue potatoes if available, but any waxy or boiling potato will work.

Heat in a small frying pan over medium heat:

1 tbsp peanut oil

Add:

½ medium onion, chopped
1 clove garlic, chopped

Cook until soft and lightly browned, 5 to 7 minutes. Transfer to a blender and add:

60g (2oz) roasted unsalted Spanish peanuts, skins removed

125ml (4floz) milk
90g (3oz) crumbled ricotta salata or curd cheese
1½ tbsp peanut oil
1 fresh jalapeño or other chilli pepper, quartered and seeded
½ tsp salt
¼ tsp ground turmeric

Blend the sauce until smooth and set aside. Cover with cold water and bring to a boil:

4-6 Peruvian blue, Yellow Finn or boiling potatoes (about 750g/1½ lb)

Cook until tender when pierced with the tip of a sharp knife, about

25 minutes. Drain and, when cool enough to handle, peel and slice into rounds.

Arrange on 4 salad plates:

Lettuce leaves

Top the lettuce with the potato slic and, if desired, season with:

Salt and ground black pepper

Spoon the reserved sauce over the potatoes. Garnish each plate with:

Hard-boiled eggs
Pickled onions
Black olives
Cooked corn on the cob, sliced into 5cm (2in) thick rounds

French Potato Salad

6 to 8 servings

Bring to a boil in a large pot with enough salted cold water to cover:

1kg (2lb) red or other waxy potatoes

Reduce the heat and simmer, uncovered, until the potatoes are tender when pierced with a fork, 20 to 25 minutes. Drain, peel if desired, and cut into bite-sized pieces. Place in a medium bowl while still warm. Whisk together in a small bowl:

6 tbsp red or white wine vinegar, or 4 tbsp white wine vinegar and 2 tbsp dry white wine
1 shallot, chopped, or ½ red onion, chopped, or 3 tbsp finely snipped fresh chives
2 tbsp chopped fresh parsley
2 tbsp drained capers (optional)
1 tbsp whole-grain mustard
1 tbsp chopped fresh tarragon, mint, dill or thyme (optional)
Salt and ground black pepper to taste

Add in a slow, steady stream, whisking constantly:

6 tbsp olive oil

Pour the dressing over the potatoes, toss gently to combine and serve warm, at room temperature, or chilled.

Tabbouleh

4 to 6 servings

Tabbouleh is a popular Middle Eastern salad.

Combine in a large bowl:

200g (6½oz) medium bulgur wheat
500ml (16floz) boiling water

Cover with an inverted plate and let stand for 30 minutes. Drain in a sieve, pressing with the back of a large spoon to remove the excess moisture, and return to the bowl. Add:

4 large ripe tomatoes, finely chopped
60g (2oz) fresh parsley sprigs, finely chopped
30g (1oz) packed fresh mint sprigs, finely chopped
30g (1oz) packed purslane, washed, dried, and finely chopped (optional)
1 bunch spring onions, finely chopped
1 medium onion, finely chopped

Stir in:

½ tsp ground allspice (optional)
½ tsp salt
¼ tsp ground black pepper

Whisk together:

5 tbsp fresh lemon juice
5 tbsp olive oil

Add to the bulgur and toss to coat. Spoon the salad onto a platter and surround with:

1 head cos lettuce, separated into leaves, washed and dried

Serve at room temperature.

Couscous Salad with Pine Nuts and Raisins

4 servings

Fine bulgur, like couscous, can also be steamed and used in this recipe.

Place in a medium bowl:

185g (6oz) quick-cook couscous

Pour in:

375ml (12floz) boiling water or stock

Cover with an inverted plate and let stand for 10 minutes. Uncover and fluff with chopsticks or a fork.

Transfer to a bowl and toss with:

60ml (2floz) *Lime Vinaigrette*, 27, prepared with cumin seeds

Add and toss to combine:

30g (1oz) pine nuts, toasted
1 yellow pepper, finely diced
6 dried apricots, finely chopped
3 tbsp sultanas
2 tbsp dried currants
2 tbsp chopped fresh coriander

QUINOA SALAD

Quinoa's taste and texture tease with lightness and a very faint herbal quality.

Prepare *Couscous Salad with Pine Nuts and Raisins, left*, substituting 280g (9oz) cooked quinoa for the couscous.

Brown Rice and Tofu Salad with Orange Sesame Dressing

6 servings

Shake together in a tightly covered jar:

125ml (4floz) rapeseed oil
4 tsp toasted sesame oil
80ml (3floz) orange juice
80ml (3floz) seasoned rice vinegar
1 small fresh jalapeño pepper, seeded and finely chopped
1 tsp chopped peeled fresh ginger
1 tsp finely chopped garlic

Chill. Combine in a large bowl:

750g (1½lb) warm cooked brown basmati rice
315g (10½oz) extra-firm tofu, pressed if desired, 80, and cut into 2cm (¾in) cubes
500g (1lb) cooked adzuki beans, rinsed and drained if tinned
60g (2oz) chopped red onions
250g (8oz) chopped peppers, preferably half red and half green
4 tbsp finely chopped fresh coriander

Shake the dressing well, pour over the rice mixture, and toss well to coat. Season with:

Salt and ground black pepper to taste

Line a serving platter with:

Lettuce leaves

Spoon the salad on the leaves and sprinkle with:

1 tbsp sesame seeds, toasted

Garlic-Sesame Triticale Salad

4 servings

A hybrid of wheat and rye, triticale berries are a little larger than wheat berries and lighter in taste.

Cook in a large pot of boiling salted water until tender, about 1 hour:

185g (6oz) triticale berries

Drain and remove to a large bowl. Heat in a small frying pan over medium heat until hot but not smoking:

3 tbsp vegetable oil

Add and cook, stirring, until very fragrant, 2 to 3 minutes:

2 spring onions, chopped
1 tbsp chopped peeled fresh ginger
1 or 2 cloves garlic, finely chopped

Stir in:

½ tsp toasted sesame oil

Salt to taste
Crushed chilli flakes to taste

Stir into the triticale berries. Taste and adjust the seasonings. Serve warm or at room temperature, garnished with:

60g (2oz) coarsely chopped dry-roasted cashews or peanuts

MAKING BEAN, RICE AND GRAIN SALADS

The mild flavours and chewy textures of beans, rice and other grains are a perfect backdrop for a variety of salads. Fresh vegetables and seasonings are added for contrast and flavour, making these versatile side dishes or healthy meals unto themselves. These salads take a bit of advance preparation, since the beans, rice and grains must first be cooked, but once made, they hold up well. If the salad has been refrigerated, let it stand at room temperature for a bit before serving, taste and adjust the seasonings (starches tend to absorb seasonings over time), and serve at room temperature. Salads are best made from beans, rice and grains that are cooked to firm-tender. Be sure everything is well drained, lest it dilute the dressing.

Rye Berry Salad with Roast Pepper Dressing

4 to 6 servings

Rye is a good source of thiamine, iron, phosphorus and potassium and has been considered a weight-loss aid because it retains water, swells more than other grains in the stomach, and digests more slowly, prolonging the feeling of fullness.

Place in a pot:

375ml (12floz) water
¼ tsp salt
125g (4oz) rye berries

Bring to a boil. Reduce the heat to low and simmer, covered, until some berries have burst and all are tender, 45 to 60 minutes.

Meanwhile, mash together to form a paste:

1 clove garlic, peeled
¼ tsp salt

Remove to a blender or food processor and add:

220g (7½oz) roast red peppers, drained
6 tbsp olive oil
2 tbsp fresh lemon juice, or to taste
2 tbsp white wine vinegar
1 shallot, chopped
1 tbsp ground cumin
Salt and ground black pepper to taste
Pinch of cayenne pepper

Purée until smooth. Drain the rye berries in a colander, transfer to a large bowl and add just enough dressing to moisten. Stir to coat. Stir in:

1 large carrot, peeled and diced
2 small celery stalks with leaves, diced
6 to 8 radishes, diced
1 medium courgette, diced
½ fennel bulb, diced
1 small yellow pepper, diced
½ small red onion, finely diced
2 tbsp chopped fresh coriander
Salt and ground black pepper to taste

Add enough additional dressing to coat. Taste and adjust the seasonings. Serve at room temperature.

Chickpea Salad

4 servings

Chickpeas are rich in vitamins A and C, high in fibre, and a good source of calcium and iron.

Combine in a medium bowl:

375g (12oz) tinned chickpeas, rinsed and drained

½ small red onion, chopped

3 tbsp chopped fresh parsley

2½ tbsp fresh lemon juice

2 tbsp extra-virgin olive oil

1 tsp creamy Dijon mustard

1-2 cloves garlic, chopped

Salt and ground black pepper to taste

On a platter, make a bed of:

315g (10oz) shredded chicory, escarole or cos lettuce, washed and dried

Spoon the chickpea salad on top and serve at room temperature.

CHICKPEA AND ROAST RED PEPPER SALAD

Prepare *Chickpea Salad*, *left*, adding 2 red peppers, roasted, *58*, peeled and diced, or 220g (7oz) roast red peppers in a jar, drained and diced, along with the onions.

Lentil and Red Potato Salad with Warm Sherry Vinaigrette

4 servings

Make this close to serving time so that it can be consumed while still warm. It goes well with braised escarole or other greens.

Cook in boiling water until tender, about 15 minutes:

375g (12oz) small red potatoes, halved if larger than 2.5cm (1in) diameter

Drain and cut into small cubes when cool enough to handle. Combine in a large bowl:

125g (4oz) thinly sliced spring onions

60g (2oz) chopped fresh parsley

Add the potato cubes along with:

375g (12oz) warm cooked green or brown lentils

Whisk together in a small saucepan:

60ml (2floz) extra-virgin olive oil

3 tbsp sherry vinegar

1 clove garlic, very finely chopped

½ tsp salt

⅛ tsp ground black pepper

Heat, stirring, until warm. Pour over the lentil mixture and serve.

White Bean Salad with Green Olives

4 to 6 servings

Serve this salad on a bed of crisp lettuce leaves, with wedges of ripe tomato and crunchy bread sticks alongside.

Combine in a medium bowl:

560g (18oz) cooked white kidney beans or other white beans, rinsed and drained if tinned

2 small celery stalks, thinly sliced

15 Spanish olives, stoned and sliced

2 tbsp chopped fresh tarragon or parsley

Whisk together:

1 tbsp red wine vinegar

1 clove garlic, finely chopped

½ tsp sweet paprika

¼ tsp salt

Whisk in:

3-4 tbsp olive oil, preferably extra-virgin

Pour the dressing over the bean mixture and toss gently to coat. Season with:

Ground black pepper to taste

Serve at room temperature.

Black Bean, Corn and Tomato Salad

6 servings

Boil in water to cover for 1 minute:

280g (9oz) sweetcorn kernels (cut from 3 ears corn)

Drain and rinse under cold water. Whisk together in a small bowl:

2 tbsp red wine vinegar

1 clove garlic, finely chopped

⅛ tsp salt

Ground black pepper to taste

Gradually whisk in:

5 tbsp olive oil, or to taste

4 tbsp snipped or sliced fresh basil

Toss with most of the dressing in a serving bowl:

560g (18oz) cooked black beans, rinsed and drained if tinned

With the remaining dressing, toss the corn along with:

250g (8oz) cherry tomatoes, halved

125g (4oz) chopped red onions

Stir gently into the beans. Serve garnished with:

Fresh basil leaves

ABOUT **SANDWICHES,** WRAPS & PIZZAS

John Montagu, an eighteenth-century diplomat and the fourth Earl of Sandwich, was an inveterate card player who disliked being taken away from his game for anything so mundane as lunch. When hunger panged, he would ask his servants for a piece of meat on top of (and perhaps also beneath) a slice of bread so he could eat without laying down his hand. Thus the sandwich got its name, and unlike so many other tales of culinary origins, this one is apparently quite true.

Even though Montagu may have been responsible for naming the sandwich, he certainly did not invent it. Almost every culture has its "sandwich", whether the burritos of Mexico, the filled pitta pockets of the Middle East or the calzones (and, by extension, pizzas — open-faced sandwiches) of Italy. Pizzas, in fact, have become a great one-dish meal all over the world.

Barbecued Aubergine and Roast Red Pepper Panini, 42

Barbecued Aubergine and Roast Red Pepper Panini

4 sandwiches

Panini *literally means "little breads", but it is a common Italian word for sandwiches.*

Prepare a medium-hot charcoal fire or preheat the grill.

Combine well:

6 fresh basil leaves, chopped
2 tbsp balsamic vinegar
1-3 cloves garlic, finely chopped
2 red peppers, roasted, 58, peeled, seeded and cut into strips about 5mm (¼ in) thick

Cut crosswise into 1cm (½in) thick slices:

1 medium aubergine

Brush the aubergine slices on both sides with:

2 tbsp olive oil

Grill the aubergine over the hot coals or grill 10cm (4in) from the heat just until tender, about 4 minutes each side. Remove from the heat. Split in half horizontally:

Four 10cm (4in) squares Focaccia, below

Spread the bottom halves generously with:

Tapenade, below

Arrange on top:

125g (4oz) sliced mozzarella, crumbled feta or goat's cheese
1 large ripe tomato, sliced

Divide the aubergine and the pepper mixture on top and cover with the top halves of the focaccia. Press together gently and serve.

Focaccia

Two 25cm (10in) focaccia

Like pizza, focaccia is essentially a large disc or slab of slightly risen bread dough – but focaccia is more bread and less topping. A simple way to make focaccia is to use pizza dough. Divide in half and roll each piece out to a 1cm (½in) thick round:

Basic pizza dough, 46

Transfer these to well-oiled 25cm (10in) cake tins. Let rise, covered with cling film, for 1½ hours. Preheat the oven to 200°C (400°F) Gas 6.

Ten minutes before baking, dimple the dough with your fingertips and drizzle evenly with:

Olive oil (as much as 125ml/4floz) – authentic focaccia is quite oily)

Top with:

Dried herbs or coarse sea salt

Bake the focaccia until golden, about 25 minutes. Remove from the tins to cool on a rack and serve warm or at room temperature.

Tapenade (Caper Olive Paste)

About 680ml (22floz)

Based on its name, the one essential ingredient in this popular spread is the caper – tapeno in Provençal. Tapenade made without capers or with only a hint of them is sometimes called olivade.

Combine in a food processor:

250g (8oz) black olives, preferably oil cured, stoned
3 tbsp drained capers

3 tbsp extra-virgin olive oil
2 tbsp brandy or fresh lemon juice
2 cloves garlic, coarsely chopped
2 tsp fresh thyme leaves, or 1 tsp dried
Salt and ground black pepper to taste

Pulse until the mixture is still coarse but of a uniform consistency.

Barbecued Vegetable Roll-Ups

4 sandwiches

Barbecue:

2 red peppers, halved

2 green peppers, halved

1 small aubergine, cut lengthwise into 1cm (½in) slices

2 medium red onions, cut into thick slices

1 courgette or summer squash, cut lengthwise into 1cm (½in) slices

8 mushrooms, wiped clean

Let stand until cool enough to handle. Chop all the barbecued vegetables into 5mm (¼in) pieces and combine in a bowl with:

2 tbsp coarsely chopped fresh basil, parsley or coriander

Salt and ground black pepper to taste

About 60ml (2floz) *Mojo*, right, or a vinaigrette of your choice, 27

Divide among:

4 flatbreads, such as pitta bread

On 2 opposite sides of the flatbread, fold over 1cm (½in), then roll up tightly, starting at one of the unfolded sides and serve.

Classic Bean Burritos

4 servings

These Mexican-American "roll-ups" differ from tacos primarily because flour rather than corn tortillas are used. Preheat the oven to 180°C (350°F) Gas 4. Divide into 2 batches and wrap in foil:

8 flour tortillas

Warm in the oven for 15 to 20 minutes. Remove from the oven and lay the tortillas flat on a work surface. Spoon down the middle of each, dividing evenly and leaving a margin of about 4cm (1½in) at the bottom edge:

750g (1½ lb) *Refried Beans*, 81

Sprinkle with:

185g (6oz) grated Gruyère

45g (1½oz) grated Cheddar cheese

60g (2oz) chopped onions

Finely chopped jalapeño or other fresh chilli peppers to taste

Fold the bottom of the tortilla up, then roll it from one side into a cylinder. Place the burritos on a baking tray and bake until the cheese is melted, about 5 minutes. Serve at once. If desired, garnish with:

Sour cream

Chopped spring onions or snipped fresh chives

GRILLED VEGETABLE BURRITOS

Prepare *Classic Bean Burritos, above,* reducing the refried beans to 185g (6oz) and omitting the cheeses, onions and peppers. Top the beans on each tortilla with about 60g (2oz) coarsely chopped mixed barbecued red peppers, courgettes and spring onions. There is no need to heat this one – just top with 1-2 tbsp fresh salsa, roll up and serve.

Mojo

About 250ml (8floz)

The national table sauce of Cuba, mojo is a colourful version of a basic vinaigrette. Traditionally made with the fresh juice of the sour orange, it can also be made with fresh lime juice and, for variation, grapefruit or pineapple juice. Unlike most vinaigrettes, mojo is briefly cooked to bring out the full flavour of the garlic. Choose plump, firm heads of cloves with tight, papery skins. Avoid cloves with brown spots or green sprouts. To chop garlic finely, slice a peeled clove lengthwise, cut through once or twice horizontally, then chop crosswise into very fine pieces.

Use caution when adding the juice to the hot oil, as it may splatter. A deep saucepan is a wise precaution. Mojo can be stored for a few days, but is best when fresh. Heat in a saucepan over medium heat:

125ml (4floz) olive oil

Add and cook until fragrant but not browned, 20 to 30 seconds:

8 cloves garlic, finely chopped

Remove from the heat and let cool 5 minutes. Carefully stir in and bring to a boil:

180ml (6floz) fresh lime, grapefruit or pineapple juice

¾ tsp ground cumin

Salt and ground black pepper to taste

Let cool and serve at room temperature. This sauce will keep, covered and refrigerated, for up to 3 days.

Falafel

4 servings

Falafel — the original "veggie burger" — is popular street food in the Middle East. The beans are soaked, ground and fried rather than boiled.

Pick over, rinse and soak, 78:

315g (10oz) dried chickpeas

Drain thoroughly. Place in a food processor and finely chop. Add:

60g (2oz) chopped onions

4 tbsp fresh parsley leaves

2 cloves garlic, chopped

2 tsp ground cumin

1½ tsp salt

**½ tsp coriander seeds, crushed, or
  ½ tsp ground coriander**

½ tsp bicarbonate of soda

¼ tsp cayenne pepper

Process until the mixture is coarsely puréed. Remove to a bowl and stir in:

2 tbsp plain flour

With wet hands, form the chickpea mixture into 4 patties, each about 7.5cm (3in) in diameter. Let stand for 15 minutes.

Meanwhile, preheat the oven to 180°C (350°F) Gas 4.

Pour into a deep frying pan:

1cm (½ in) vegetable oil

Fry the chickpea patties until golden on both sides, about 4 minutes each side. Drain on paper towels. Stir together:

60ml (2floz) tahini

60ml (2floz) cold water

1 tbsp fresh lemon juice

Pinch of salt

Wrap in foil:

4 pitta breads

Heat in the oven until warmed, about 10 minutes. Open one edge of each pitta bread and distribute among the pockets:

**125g (4oz) thinly sliced crisp
  lettuce (such as cos or iceberg),
  washed and dried**

4 thin tomato slices

Add a falafel to each pitta and drizzle the tahini sauce over the falafel. Add:

Tabasco sauce to taste

Hummus (Middle Eastern Chickpea and Sesame Dip)

About 500ml (16floz)

If using tinned chickpeas, rinse 500g (16oz) and purée as directed, using water to thin the purée. In Egypt, hummus is flavoured with cumin; use ½ tsp ground cumin for this quantity.

Pick over, rinse, and soak, 78:

185g (6oz) dried chickpeas

Drain and place in a pan with water to cover by 5cm (2in). Bring to a boil, reduce the heat and simmer until very tender, about 1½ hours. Drain, reserving the cooking liquid. Remove the chickpeas to a food processor or blender and add:

80ml (3floz) fresh lemon juice
3 tbsp tahini
2 cloves garlic, finely chopped
Salt to taste

Purée until smooth, adding 2 to 3 tbsp of the cooking liquid as needed to obtain a soft, creamy consistency. Remove to a shallow serving bowl and garnish with:

1 tbsp olive oil
1 tbsp finely chopped fresh parsley
Sprinkling of hot or sweet paprika

Serve with:

Warm pitta bread

Baba Ghanoush (Roast Aubergine Dip)

About 500ml (16floz)

You can stir 125g (4oz) yoghurt into the aubergine purée just before serving, then garnish.

Preheat the oven to 200°C (400°F) Gas 6.

Pierce in several places:

3 medium aubergines (about 2kg/4lb)

Roast on a baking tray until the skins are dark mahogany in colour and the flesh feels soft, 45 to 60 minutes. Let stand until cool enough to handle. Split the aubergines and scoop the flesh into a colander. Press lightly to extract the excess liquid. Remove to a food processor and add:

1½ tbsp tahini
2 cloves garlic, chopped
Juice of 1 large lemon
½ tsp salt

Pulse until smooth. Taste and adjust the seasonings. Remove to a shallow serving bowl and garnish with:

1 tbsp olive oil
1 tbsp finely chopped fresh parsley
Several stoned black olives (optional)

Serve with:

Warm pitta bread

Whipped Feta with Roast Peppers

About 500ml (16floz)

Combine in a food processor:

500g (1lb) Greek feta cheese, crumbled
2 tbsp extra-virgin olive oil

Pulse until the feta is creamy. Add:

1 red pepper, roasted, 58, peeled, seeded and coarsely chopped
2 or 3 fresh jalapeño peppers, seeded and chopped
2 pickled pepperoncini, rinsed, seeded and chopped
Several grindings of black pepper

Pulse until the mixture is well combined while gradually adding:

3 tbsp extra-virgin olive oil
2 tbsp fresh lemon juice

The feta should be creamy and spreadable. Taste and add more olive oil and/or lemon juice if desired. Serve with:

Crackers or pitta bread

PEPPERONCINI

These sweet to mildly piquant pale green to red peppers are best known as a pickled pepper used in Italian dishes. They are rarely found fresh in markets but are popular with many home gardeners. They measure about 7.5cm (3in) long and 2cm (¾in) wide at the stem end, sloping gently to a point.

Pizza with Tomato Sauce and Mozzarella

Two 30cm (12in) pizzas

This pizza has a relatively thick crust. We advise not overloading your pizza with sauce and cheese.

Combine in a large mixing bowl or the bowl of a heavy-duty mixer and let stand until the yeast is dissolved, about 5 minutes:

1 packet (2¼ tsp) active dried yeast
330ml (11floz) warm (40°-46°C/ 105°-115°F) water

Add:

500-525g (1lb-1lb 2oz) plain flour
2 tbsp olive oil
1 tbsp salt
1 tbsp sugar (optional)

Mix by hand or on low speed for about 1 minute to blend all the ingredients. Knead for about 10 minutes by hand or with the dough hook on low to medium speed until the dough is smooth and elastic. Transfer the dough to a bowl lightly coated with olive oil and turn it over once to coat with oil. Cover with cling film and let rise in a warm place (23°-26°C/ 75°-80°F) until doubled in volume, 1 to 1½ hours.

Preheat the oven to 240°C (475°F) Gas 8½. Grease and dust 2 baking trays with cornmeal; or place a baking stone (if you have one) in the oven and preheat it for 45 minutes. Punch the dough down and divide it in half. Roll each piece into a ball and let rest, loosely covered with cling film, for 10 to 15 minutes.

Flatten each ball of dough 1 at a time on a lightly floured work surface into a 30cm (12in) round, rolling and stretching the dough. Place each dough circle on a prepared baking tray; if using a baking stone, place them on baker's peels dusted with cornmeal. Lift the edge and pinch it to form a lip. To prevent the filling making the crust soggy, brush the top of the dough with:

Olive oil

Use your fingertips to push dents in the surface of the dough (to prevent bubbling) and let rest for about 10 minutes. Spread in an even layer on each pizza, leaving a 1cm (½in) border:

125ml (4floz) Italian Tomato Sauce, right

Sprinkle each with:

185g (6oz) mozzarella, grated

If using a baking stone, slide the pizza off the baker's peel onto the stone in the preheated oven. If making the pizza on a baking tray, place the pan and pizza in the oven on the bottom rack. Bake until the crust is browned and the cheese is golden, about 12 minutes. Remove from the oven, slice and serve at once.

PIZZA WITH FENNEL, ONION AND ASIAGO CHEESE

Prepare dough as above, and spread with Italian Tomato Sauce, right, *before adding this topping.*

Sauté 1 medium onion, sliced; 1 fennel bulb, trimmed and sliced; and 2 cloves garlic, finely chopped, in 2 tbsp olive oil along with ½ tsp dried marjoram and ¼ tsp crushed chilli flakes until the onions are translucent, 5 to 7 minutes. Spread evenly over the pizzas. Season to taste with salt and ground black pepper and bake as directed. Five minutes before the pizza is done, sprinkle 45g (1½oz) grated Asiago cheese over the top.

Italian Tomato Sauce

This classic tomato sauce can be kept in the refrigerator for up to 4 days or frozen for up to 3 months. It puts ripe garden tomatoes to excellent use.

Heat in a large frying pan over medium heat:

2-3 tbsp extra-virgin olive oil

Add:

5 tbsp finely chopped fresh parsley
1 medium onion, finely chopped
1 small carrot, peeled and finely chopped
1 celery stalk with leaves, finely chopped

Cook, stirring, until the onions are golden brown, about 5 minutes.

Add:

2 cloves garlic, finely chopped
30g (1oz) fresh basil leaves, chopped, or 1 sprig each fresh rosemary, sage and thyme

Cook, stirring, for about 30 seconds.

Stir in:

1.25kg (2½lb) ripe tomatoes, peeled, if desired, seeded, and coarsely chopped, or three 400g (14oz) tins whole tomatoes, with juice, crushed between your fingers as you add them to the pan
1 tbsp tomato purée (optional)
Salt and ground black pepper to taste

Simmer, uncovered, until the sauce is thickened, about 10 minutes. Remove the herb sprigs.

Calzone with Portobello Mushrooms and Goat's Cheese

2 calzones; 4 servings

Calzone, literally "pant leg", is a pizza folded onto itself – a closed envelope of dough with the toppings on the inside.
Prepare through the first rise:
Basic pizza dough, opposite
Preheat the oven to 230°C (450°F) Gas 8. Lightly grease a baking tray. Divide the dough in half and form each half into a ball. Place on a lightly floured work surface, sprinkle with flour and cover with a tea towel or cling film. Let stand for 20 minutes.
Meanwhile, sauté until tender:
1 tbsp olive oil
2 large portobello mushrooms, thinly sliced
8-10 button mushrooms, thinly sliced
1 red onion, thinly sliced
3 cloves garlic, finely chopped
Let cool and season with:
Salt and ground black pepper to taste
Shape each ball of dough into a thick disc and let stand for about 5 minutes. Roll each one into a 25cm (10in) round. Divide the filling between the rounds. Sprinkle evenly with:
½ tsp dried thyme
125g (4oz) goat's cheese, crumbled
Fold the dough over, making a half circle, and tightly seal the edges with your fingertips. Reduce the oven temperature to 200°C (400°F) Gas 6. Place the calzones on the baking tray and bake until nicely browned, 30 to 35 minutes. Serve hot or at room temperature.

White Pizza with Potatoes and Sage

Two 30cm (12in) pizzas

According to some labelling laws, if it does not have tomato sauce, you cannot call it pizza. This would astonish some Italians, who frequently eat their pizza with just a touch of tomato or even none at all.
Prepare as directed:
Basic pizza dough, opposite
Brush each generously with:
Extra-virgin olive oil
Top each with:
250g (8oz) potatoes, boiled and very thinly sliced while still warm
2 tsp dried or 2 tbsp coarsely chopped fresh sage
2 tbsp extra-virgin olive oil
Salt and ground black pepper to taste
If using a baking stone, slide the pizza off the baker's peel onto the baking stone in the preheated oven. If making the pizza on a baking tray, place the pan and pizza in the oven on the bottom rack. Bake until the crust is golden brown, about 12 minutes. Remove from the oven, slice and serve at once.

Barbecued Pizza with Tomato and Three Cheeses

One 25-30cm (10-12in) pizza

Barbecuing pizza requires a hot fire started with kindling and fuelled with hardwood charcoal. Build your fire on one side of the barbecue. For cooking, you will want a cool area on the barbecue in order to add the toppings without burning the bottom of the crust. For kettle-type barbecues, create a centre line with two or three bricks laid end to end and bank the charcoal on one side. If your barbecue cannot accommodate a 30cm (12in) round of dough, simply divide the dough and make 2 or 3 small pizzas. Set up your work area as close to the barbecue as possible. The dough, olive oil and a variety of topping ingredients should be close at hand and ready before you begin. This recipe will serve four as a first course or one as a main course. The dough can easily be doubled or tripled.

Combine in a mixing bowl or in the bowl of a heavy-duty mixer:

1 tsp active dry yeast
2 tbsp warm (40-46°C/ 105-115°F) water

Let stand until the yeast is dissolved and the water is foamy on the surface, about 5 minutes. Add:

160ml (5floz) cool water
315g (10oz) unbleached plain flour
1½ tsp coarse salt

Mix until the dough comes together. Knead by hand or with the dough hook on medium speed until the dough is smooth and elastic, about 10 minutes. Brush a large bowl with:

Olive oil

Add the dough and brush the surface with:

Olive oil

Cover the bowl with cling film and let rise in a warm place away from draughts until doubled in volume, about 2 hours. Punch the dough down. Cover with cling film and let rise for at least 45 minutes at room temperature or overnight in the refrigerator.

While the dough is rising, prepare a hot charcoal fire, setting the barbecue rack 7.5-10cm (3-4in) above the coals. Prepare the topping ingredients. Brush a large flat baking sheet with:

1 tbsp olive oil

Place 1 ball of dough on the sheet and turn it over to coat with oil. With your hands, spread and flatten the pizza dough into a 25-30cm (10-12in) freeform circle, 5mm (¼ in) thick. You may end up with a rectangle rather than a circle; the shape is unimportant. If the dough shrinks back into itself, let it stand for a few minutes, then continue to spread and flatten the dough. Do not make a lip. Take care not to stretch the dough so thin that it tears. If this happens, all is not lost; rather than try to repair the holes, simply avoid them when adding the toppings. When the fire is hot (you will be able to hold your hand 13cm/5in) above the fire for only 3 to 4 seconds), use your fingertips to lift the dough gently by the 2 corners closest to you and drape it onto the coolest part of the rack. Catch the loose edge on the barbecue first and guide the remaining dough into place over the fire. Cover, and within 2 to 3 minutes, the dough will puff slightly, the underside will stiffen and grill marks will appear. Using spring-loaded tongs and a metal spatula, immediately flip the crust over onto the coolest part of the

barbecue. Quickly brush the grilled surface with:

2 tsp olive oil

Spread over the surface of the pizza:

4 tbsp grated Parmesan cheese
30g (1oz) grated fontina cheese
2 tbsp grated pecorino cheese

Spoon in dollops on top:

6 tbsp chopped tinned tomatoes in tomato sauce

Top with:

1 tbsp chopped fresh parsley
1 tsp ground black pepper

Sprinkle on top:

1-2 tbsp olive oil

After the toppings have been added, slide the pizza back towards the hot coals so that about half of the pizza is directly over the heat. Rotate the pizza frequently so that different sections receive high heat and check the underside by lifting the edge with tongs to be sure it is not burning. The pizza is done when the top is bubbling and the cheese is melted. Garnish with:

5 fresh basil leaves, torn by hand

Serve immediately.

MIXED HERBS AND CHEESE PIZZA

Liberally brush the cooked side of the pizza with olive oil. Top with 45g (1½ oz) grated fontina cheese, 2 tbsp grated pecorino cheese, ½ tsp finely chopped fresh garlic, 4 tbsp chopped mixed fresh herbs (oregano, thyme, basil, rosemary) and 4 tbsp chopped fresh parsley. Drizzle 2 to 3 tbsp olive oil over the top. Finish barbecuing as directed.

ABOUT
VEGETABLES

*I*t is a glorious time for vegetable lovers. Farmers at their markets, exporters and seedsmen are showering us with tastes, textures and aromas we had never even heard of a few years ago. Science keeps confirming the age-old maternal admonition to eat your vegetables. The specific diseases you can avoid and the miracle micronutrient of the moment might change with each new study, but the general consensus stays the same: vegetables are good for you. Every vegetable contains every nutrient — every vitamin (with the exception of vitamin B_{12}, which vegetarians can obtain easily from dairy products), every mineral, every kind of dietary fibre. It is less important to worry about which vegetable has the higher amount of one vitamin or antioxidant than to eat as many vegetables as you can, the fresher the better.

June Vegetable Ragout, 75

Buying and Keeping Fresh Vegetables

Avoid vegetables that look dry or wrinkled, bruised or badly blemished. If two vegetables are of equal size and one is heavier, the heavier vegetable, which retains more moisture, will be more succulent. A good rule to follow is to select vegetables as close to the same size as possible – this ensures even cooking, even when pieces are cut up.

Because vegetables are generally less fragile than fruits, they are permitted to ripen before harvest. Fresh vegetables are still very much alive when you bring them into the kitchen. A cold, moist environment helps keep their tissues vibrant. For most vegetables, the shelter of a sealed perforated plastic bag in a closed refrigerator crisper is ideal. However, if there is too much moisture, tissues start to deteriorate. For this reason, wait until just before cooking them to wash vegetables.

Here are a few points for storing fresh vegetables. **Buds and stems:** Plunge the stalks of artichokes, asparagus, broccoli and cauliflower and any long-stemmed greens in a jug of water, then refrigerate. **Greens without stems:** Whether for salad or cooking, wrap in barely moist paper towels, then place in a perforated vegetable bag. **Roots:** Cut off any greens on top, leaving 5-7.5cm (2-3in) of stems. Wrap the greens separately. Leaves draw moisture from their roots – an advantage for the leaves, but not the roots. **Mushrooms:** Wrap these in a loose paper bag.

If the vegetable comes wrapped in cellophane, remove the wrapper and place the vegetable in a perforated plastic bag. The following vegetables are best stored in a cool, dry place – ideally somewhere between 7 and 10°C (45 and 50°F), but a warmer temperature is better than a colder one: aubergines, garlic, onions, plantains, potatoes, winter squash, sweet potatoes, taro roots, tomatoes, yams and cassavas (yuca roots).

Preparing Vegetables

Prepare vegetables as close to cooking time as possible. All vegetables grown commercially and most you grow yourself – even organically raised vegetables – should be washed before preparing. Only the insides of layered vegetables (lettuces, cabbages, onions) can be presumed to be free of dust and the errant insect. Wash vegetables no more than is needed to remove dust and dirt. Root vegetables whose peel you will retain should be scrubbed with a fairly stiff brush – you can see the soil melt away. Do not use a woven plastic or metal pad to scrub vegetables, as brittle bits of the pad can break off and get buried, unseen, in the food. In bunches of greens where soil gathers at the base, cut off the base, separate the leaves, and drop them into a sinkful of tepid, not cold, water. Tepid water relaxes the leaves just enough for them to let down hidden grains of sand. Swish gently with your hands. Individual leaves such as those of mustard greens can be rinsed individually. Lift the greens into a colander; empty the water and check for sand at the bottom of the sink; rinse the sink and repeat until the bottom is clean. With some greens, it will be necessary to repeat several times.

If you suspect the vegetable has been treated with wax and/or pesticide, the best approach is to wash it, peel it and wash it again. Pesticide residue cannot be washed off most vegetables. Guidelines for peeling and cutting vegetables vary by vegetable type. Information on both procedures follows.

Peeling Vegetables

The skin is a vegetable's seal, keeping nutrients in and microorganisms out. Break that seal – do whatever cutting and slicing is needed – as close to cooking as possible. If necessary, vegetables can be cut up and refrigerated in an airtight container several hours in advance. Packaged precut vegetables such as carrot sticks usually have been treated with an antispoilage solution, and sensitive palates can taste it. Leave the skin on a vegetable whenever possible, unless you suspect it has been sprayed or waxed. The most efficient tool for peeling thin skin is a carbon-steel swivel-bladed peeler, which keeps its sharp edge over time; supermarket swivel-bladed peelers are fine but should be replaced every few months. Pare as thinly as possible. A paring knife invariably takes more flesh of the vegetable along with it than is necessary. If the vegetable is cooked whole and then peeled and sliced, maximum nutrients and flavour are retained, and the skin is easier to remove.

A few vegetables, notably potatoes, artichokes, salsify, celeriac, Jerusalem artichokes and some tropical roots, darken when their flesh is exposed to air. With these vegetables use only a stainless-steel blade – carbon steel will react with the flesh and darken it instantly. Darkened flesh is harmless, but to prevent susceptible flesh from discolouring, drop the pared vegetable into cold water mixed with lemon or lime juice or vinegar (1 tbsp juice or vinegar to 1 litre/1½ pints water) for no more than 20 minutes, lest nutrients and flavour start leaching out.

HOW TO CHOP AN ONION

When chopping onions, tears can be reduced by chilling onions before peeling, or by peeling them under running water. To peel, use the tip of a sharp paring knife to pull the skin off the onion, then pull off any membrane underneath. Some cooks opt to chop onions in the food processor, but hand chopping keeps pieces drier and more uniform in shape. Cutting an onion chef's style keeps pieces from scattering all over the board and gives you control of the size of the pieces.

1 Halve the peeled onion lengthwise. Lay the halves cut side down on the board. Steady the piece lightly with the tips of the fingers of your assisting hand (the rest of your hand safely turned under, so just the first joints of the hand are exposed to the knife). Slice the onion lengthwise in parallel cuts up to, but not through, the root. (For slices, now cut off the root.)

2 Next, make several horizontal cuts of the desired thickness parallel to the board up to, but not through, the root. (For matchsticks, now cut off the root.)

3 For diced or chopped pieces, cut through the onion at right angles to the last cuts at the desired thickness, then cut through the root.

Cutting Vegetables

For uniform pieces that will finish cooking at the same time, cut by hand, with the slicing disk on a food processor, or with a mandoline. When a vegetable has two parts with distinctly different shapes and textures, as broccoli does, you must cut the denser, slower-cooking part into smaller pieces than the more tender part if both are to cook in the same amount of time. The same is true when cooking two or more vegetables together, as when steaming swedes and potatoes before mashing them. Chop them into pieces – the swedes slightly smaller, as they take a little longer to cook than potatoes – and arrange them in the steamer. Another reason for cutting vegetables is to expose just the right amount of surface to the seasoning you have in mind.

All hand cutting begins with slicing. Many chopping and slicing devices are available, but nothing can replace a skilled, relaxed wrist and a sharp, heavy knife. Practise with a mushroom, which is yielding and not slippery when placed cap down,

and work up to an onion, which can be both resistant and evasive.

The point of the knife is never lifted from the chopping board; instead it forms a pivot. The knife handle is raised high enough to be eased gently up and down, its wide blade guided by the perpendicular forefinger and midfinger of the free hand, which holds and guides the vegetable being cut. As the slicing progresses, inch a slow retreat with the free hand, which should keep a firm grasp on the object. When roll-cutting, make a diagonal cut straight down, roll the carrot (or turnip or potato) a quarter turn, and slice again. Repeat until all of the carrot is cut.

It is easier to slice a round vegetable, like a potato, if you first cut a thin slice off the bottom to create a flat surface to rest on the chopping board (the resulting slices will not be completely round, however). For attractive diagonal slices of a thin vegetable, such as green beans or asparagus, hold the knife at an angle to either the vegetable or

the chopping board. For most everyday cooking, vegetables are simply sliced crosswise; they can first be cut lengthwise into halves or quarters if they are very thick. But if you want to turn slices into more elegant strips or cubes, cut long vegetables, like courgettes, into 5cm (2in) chunks and then slice the pieces lengthwise (for the tidiest appearance, first cut a straight edge on all sides of the chunks and discard the scraps – or save them for the stockpot). Round vegetables, like turnips, can be sliced crosswise or lengthwise, depending on which will yield the longer slice.

To cut slices into smaller pieces, stack them, a few at a time, then cut them into very thin strips (less than 3mm/⅛in) to make a julienne, slightly wider strips (about 3mm/⅛in) to make matchsticks, or much wider strips (about 5mm/¼in) to make batons. To dice the vegetable, cut first into 1cm (½in) strips, then hold them together and cut across them to make 1cm (½in) cubes or tiny 3mm (⅛in) cubes.

Chard Sautéed with Garlic

4 to 6 servings

Remove the stems from:

2 medium bunches red or green chard (about 750g/½ lb)

Cut the stems into 1cm (½in) pieces. Coarsely chop the leaves; rinse well, but do not dry. Heat in a large frying pan over medium-low heat until the oil smells good and the garlic is just beginning to colour:

2 tbsp extra-virgin olive oil
2 cloves garlic, thinly sliced
1 small dried red chilli pepper, crumbled, or ¼ to ½ tsp crushed chilli flakes (optional)

Add the chard stems and season with:

Salt to taste

Cook, stirring occasionally, until the stems are nearly tender, about 2 minutes. Add the chard leaves and cook, partially covered, until both the leaves and the stems are tender, 3 to 5 minutes more. Season with:

Juice of ½ lemon or 1½ tbsp red wine vinegar

Taste again for salt. Serve in a bowl, surrounded with:

Lemon wedges

Sautéed Broccoli with Garlic and Crushed Chilli Flakes

4 servings

A southern Italian way of preparing all kinds of vegetables. You can toss the cooked broccoli with pasta, stoned black olives and grated Parmesan or pecorino cheese to make a main course.
Remove the florets, then peel and dice the stems of:
1kg (2lb) broccoli
Steam or boil until barely tender, then drain. If not finishing the dish until later, cool the broccoli under cold running water. Heat in a large frying pan:
3 tbsp extra-virgin olive oil
Add and cook, stirring over medium heat until their aromas are released:
2 cloves garlic, thinly sliced or chopped
2 good pinches of crushed chilli flakes or 1 small dried red chilli pepper, crumbled
Add the broccoli and cook until heated through and tender, 3 to 4 minutes longer. Season with:
Salt and ground black pepper to taste

Sautéed Tiny New Potatoes

4 servings

Watch your local market for the first little new potatoes arriving around July.
Scrub well and pat dry:
24 very small new potatoes, about the same size
Heat in a large, heavy frying pan:
2 tbsp olive oil or 30g (1oz) clarified butter
Roll the potatoes around the pan to coat them, then cover and cook over low heat until tender, about 25 minutes. Every so often give the pan a gentle shake so that they brown evenly. Sprinkle with:
Salt and ground black pepper to taste
Snipped fresh chives, chopped fresh parsley, or other fresh herb (optional)

Stir-Fry of Chinese Cabbage and Carrots

4 servings

Heat a wok or large frying pan over high heat. Add and stir-fry for a few seconds, but do not allow the garlic to brown:
1 tbsp peanut or vegetable oil
2 cloves garlic, finely chopped
1 tbsp chopped peeled fresh ginger
Add and stir-fry for 3 minutes:
250g (8oz) carrots, grated
Then add and stir-fry until the cabbage is tender, about 3 more minutes:
1 medium-large head Chinese cabbage (about 1kg/2lb), rinsed and thinly sliced
Add and stir well to mix:
2 tbsp light or dark soy sauce
1 tsp toasted sesame oil
½ tsp chilli paste with garlic or ¼ tsp red pepper flakes (optional)
Serve immediately, sprinkled with:
Chopped fresh coriander or parsley

STIR-FRYING

Vegetables cut in small, even pieces and stirred over intensely high heat with a modicum of fat and liquid cook through in the fastest possible time. Stir-frying is most efficient when the pieces of food have plenty of room to move in the pan, allowing surfaces constant exposure to heat. Work in several batches, if necessary, to prevent vegetables from being crowded and steaming in their own moisture, which prevents browning and dilutes flavour. Many vegetables are best stir-fried until golden or brown and then finished with steam by adding liquid and covering the pan. This method reduces the amount of fat needed and yields excellent taste. For best results, the vegetables should be sliced to uniform thickness. Cut those that tend to stringiness on a diagonal. Stem ends and midribs should be removed from coarse-leaf vegetables, then sliced and cooked separately. Use 1 to 2 tbsp cooking oil – peanut oil is a great favourite – per 500g (1lb) of vegetables.

Stir-Fried Bok Choy with Mushrooms

4 to 6 servings

Place in a small bowl:

6 dried shiitake mushrooms

Pour over the mushrooms:

125ml (4floz) boiling water

Let soak for 20 minutes, stirring the mushrooms occasionally. While the mushrooms soak, prepare, keeping the stems separate from the leafy parts:

750g-1kg (1½ -2lb) bok choy, bottoms trimmed, stalks washed and cut into 5cm (2in) pieces

In a small saucepan, warm over medium-low heat:

250ml (8floz) *Vegetable Stock, 17*

½ tsp salt

½ tsp sugar

Remove the mushrooms from their soaking liquid and reserve the liquid. Cut the mushrooms into 5mm (¼in) slices and set aside. In a small bowl, mix:

2 tbsp reserved mushroom soaking liquid, strained

1 tbsp Scotch whisky or Shaoxing wine

2 tsp cornflour

¾ tsp ground white pepper

Heat in a wok or a large frying pan over high heat:

3 tbsp peanut oil

Add the reserved mushrooms and bok choy stems and cook, stirring often, for 3 to 5 minutes to soften. Add the reserved bok choy leaves and warmed vegetable stock, cover, and steam until the leaves wilt, 1 to 2 minutes. Uncover and transfer the vegetables with a slotted spoon to a serving dish. Stir the reserved cornflour mixture and whisk into the stock. Bring to a boil, whisking, and add:

2 tsp toasted sesame oil

Stir well, pour the sauce over the vegetables and serve.

Stir-Fried Yard-Long Beans with Ginger and Garlic

4 servings

Yard-long beans keep their firm-crunchy texture when stir-fried. Select thin, dark green beans – as opposed to the lighter-coloured beans – for best flavour.
Heat a wok over high heat for 30 seconds. Add:

2 tbsp peanut oil

Swirl the wok to coat it with the oil and heat until the oil is hot. Add:

500g (1lb) yard-long beans or green beans, trimmed and cut to the desired length

1 tbsp chopped peeled fresh ginger

2 tsp finely chopped fresh garlic

¼ tsp salt, or to taste

Stir-fry until the beans are bright green, 5 to 6 minutes. Do not allow the garlic to burn. Add:

3-4 tbsp rich stock or water

Cover and simmer gently until the beans are tender, 8 to 10 minutes.

Roasting Peppers

Roasting provides the best way to remove the skin of peppers. In addition, it softens their flesh, tempers the raw taste and adds a delicious smokiness. Thick-walled peppers can be taken a step further and charred. Thinner-walled peppers – this includes most chillies – are better if blistered but not completely charred, or they will lose flesh when you peel them. Red peppers tend to char faster than green ones, having more sugars in their flesh. Once they are blistered, lay peppers in a bowl and cover with a tea towel, plate or cling film. Leave for a few minutes. Their heat will create steam, which will loosen the skins. Try not to rinse peppers after roasting, for much of the smoky flavour is on the surface.

Scrape off the skins with a knife. If the peppers were whole, make a slit down one side, then run the tip of a small serrated knife around the stem underneath its base. Remove the top and the core and seeds that come with it, then scrape away remaining seeds and cut away the membranes. Add any juices in the bottom of the bowl to the dish you are making, or blend them into a vinaigrette dressing. Roasting and peeling can be done a day or two in advance; wrap the peppers airtight and refrigerate.

Stove-Roasting Fresh Peppers: This is the simplest method. Place whole peppers directly in the flames of your gas burner on its highest setting. Keep an eye on the peppers and turn them frequently with tongs, letting the peppers blister or char (do not pierce with a cooking fork, as juices will be lost). Continue until the entire surface is blistered.

Many cooks quickly stove-roast dried chilli peppers before rehydrating them. A flash of intense heat deepens and rounds out flavours.

Grill-Roasting Fresh Peppers: Line a grill pan with foil. Place whole peppers on the foil and brush with olive oil. Grill, turning as needed, until blackened on all sides.

Barbecue-Roasting Fresh Peppers: This is the most flavourful method for roasting peppers. Set whole peppers on a rack over ash-covered coals, a hot but dying fire. Let them sit in one place until they are blistered or charred, then turn them and repeat until the whole pepper is done.

Grill- or Pan-Roasting Fresh Peppers: This is for small fresh chillies such as serranos and jalapeños. Heat a dry cast-iron grill pan or frying pan over high heat, add the whole peppers, and shake them around the pan until their skins are soft and charred here and there. These chillies are customarily not peeled after roasting, but can be.

Roast Portobello Mushrooms, Fines Herbes

About 4 servings

Brief high-heat roasting draws out just enough moisture to intensify the good flavour of these fine mushrooms. Any large, thick, fleshy caps roast successfully – thin mushrooms can turn leathery. Choose clean caps – water can be absorbed by the tissues, diluting the flavour.

Position a rack in the centre of the oven. Preheat the oven to 260°C (500°F) Gas 9.

Gently wipe the tops of:

Four 125g (4oz) portobello or 500g (1lb) chestnut mushrooms

Trim off the stems at the caps (save for another use). Brush the bottom of a rimmed baking tray and the tops of the caps with:

About 60g (2oz) unsalted butter, melted, or 4 tbsp olive oil

Arrange the caps rounded side up in the pan and roast for 6 minutes.

Remove from the oven, closing the oven door, and quickly turn the caps over with tongs, rearranging chestnut mushrooms, if using, in the pan. Sprinkle with:

30g (1oz) unsalted butter, melted, or 2 tbsp olive oil
Salt and ground black pepper to taste

Return to the oven and roast until the caps look evenly roasted, 5 to 6 minutes more. Serve as a first course on small hot plates, rounded side up, drizzled with pan juices (if any) and sprinkled with a portion of the following mixture:

1 tbsp chopped fresh chives
1 tbsp chopped fresh chervil
1 tbsp chopped fresh parsley
1 tbsp chopped spring onions
1 tbsp chopped fresh tarragon

PREPARING MUSHROOMS

Clean mushrooms with a soft brush or wipe with a damp cloth. Or if the mushrooms are truly grimy, rinse them quickly under cold running water and pat dry. Never soak mushrooms – their delicate tissues will absorb water. If desired, slice 3mm (⅛in) off the bottom of the stems to refresh them but do not discard the flavourful stems. If only caps are called for in a recipe, cut the stem flush with the cap. Either chop the stems fairly fine, toss them until lightly browned in a little butter, and add them to the dish or use within a day to flavour something else. As a general rule, use intense heat – sauté, stir-fry, grill, barbecue – when cooking mushrooms, and cook just enough to brown them lightly and heat them through.

Roast Potatoes, Beetroot and Onions Vinaigrette

6 servings

Preheat the oven to 190°C (375°F) Gas 5.

Toss together and arrange in a single layer in a baking tin:

12 medium red potatoes, halved or quartered lengthwise
12 cloves garlic, unpeeled
2 tbsp olive oil
Fresh rosemary or thyme sprigs
Salt and ground black pepper to taste

Toss together and arrange in another baking pan:

250g (8oz) baby onions, peeled

1 tbsp olive oil
Salt and ground black pepper to taste

Toss together and arrange in a third baking tin:

375g (12oz) baby red or golden beetroot, trimmed and scrubbed
1 tbsp olive oil
Salt and ground black pepper to taste

Tightly cover each tin with foil and roast the vegetables until tender, 35 to 40 minutes; uncover the potatoes and garlic after 20 minutes

to allow them to brown and crisp slightly. Reserve any juices from the beetroot and onions and stir into:

Basic Vinaigrette, 27

While the beetroot is still warm, gently rub their skins off, using paper towels. Arrange the roasted vegetables around a mound of:

30g (1oz) mixed fresh herbs

Drizzle the vinaigrette over the vegetables. Serve at room temperature.

Ratatouille

4 to 6 servings

This Provençal vegetable mélange can be served warm as a main course with saffron rice.

Sauté in a large frying pan or flameproof casserole over high heat until the vegetables are golden and just tender, 10 to 12 minutes:

60ml (2floz) olive oil

1 medium aubergine (about 500g/1lb), peeled and cut into 2.5cm (1in) cubes

500g (1lb) courgettes, cut into 2.5cm (1in) cubes

Remove the vegetables and reduce the heat to medium-high. In the same pan, cook until the onions are slightly softened:

2 tbsp olive oil

185g (6oz) sliced onions

Add and cook, stirring occasionally, until the vegetables are just tender but not browned, 8 to 12 minutes:

2 large red peppers, cut into 2.5cm (1in) squares

3 cloves garlic, chopped

Season with:

Salt and ground black pepper to taste

Add:

280g (9oz) chopped, seeded, peeled fresh tomatoes

2-3 sprigs fresh thyme

1 bay leaf

Reduce the heat to low, cover and cook for 5 minutes. Add the aubergine and courgette and cook until everything is tender, about 20 minutes more. Taste and adjust the seasonings. Stir in:

4 tbsp chopped fresh basil

HOW TO PEEL AND SEED TOMATOES

1 To peel tomatoes, cut a small X in the bottom of each one – do not cut the flesh.

2 Ease the tomatoes one by one into a pot of boiling water. Leave ripe tomatoes in for about 15 seconds, barely ripe tomatoes in for twice as long. Lift the tomatoes out with a sieve and drop into a bowl of iced water to stop the cooking. Pull off the skin with the tip of the knife. If the skin sticks, return the tomato to the boiling water for another 10 seconds and repeat. If the dish can use a touch of smoky flavour and if you have a gas burner, an easier way to peel tomatoes is to hold the tomato on a long-handled fork over the burner, turning it until the skin splits. Do not plunge the tomatoes in water, but after cooling, peel as above.

3 To seed and juice tomatoes, cut each one crosswise in half (between the top and bottom). Squeeze each half gently, cut side down, over a sieve set in a bowl. Now run the tip of a finger into each of the cavities and flick out the mass of seeds.

Root Vegetable Purée

4 to 6 servings

The potatoes lend this purée a light texture and delicate flavour.

Place in a large saucepan:

250g (8oz) boiling or baking potatoes, peeled and thinly sliced

Add water to cover generously, bring to a boil, and cook for 5 minutes. Add:

500g (1lb) carrots, peeled, halved and cut into thick slices

Continue cooking until both vegetables are completely tender, about 25 minutes. Drain and return the vegetables to the pan. Working over low heat, mash the vegetables with a potato masher or beat with a hand-held mixer until very smooth.

Mix in:

125ml (4floz) milk or cream
20g (¾ oz) butter, softened
½ tsp salt
¼ tsp ground white pepper

Taste and adjust the seasonings and cook just until heated through. Serve piping hot. If desired, top with:

Cress Butter, right

CELERIAC PURÉE

Prepare *Root Vegetable Purée, above,* substituting 2 medium celeriac (about 750g/1½ lb total), peeled, quartered and thinly sliced, for the carrots. Flavour with a little Dijon mustard and chopped fresh thyme or snipped fresh chives.

Cress Butter

About 60g (2oz)

Wonderfully zippy with root vegetables. In a small bowl, cream with a fork or wooden spoon:

60g (2oz) butter (preferably unsalted), softened

Gradually stir in:

1½ tsp finely chopped watercress
Dash of lemon juice
Salt and ground white pepper to taste

Roll the mixture into a cylinder in a piece of greaseproof paper, cling film or foil (or shape as desired), and refrigerate or freeze until firm enough to slice. Or refrigerate in a small bowl or ramekin and spoon on just before serving.

Courgette Pancakes with Mint and Feta Cheese

About 19 pancakes; 6 to 8 servings

Shred on the large holes of a grater or in a food processor:

1.25kg (2½ lb) green or yellow courgettes

Sprinkle lightly with:

Salt

Mix together in a bowl:

2 large eggs

125g (4oz) crumbled feta cheese

45g (1½ oz) dry breadcrumbs

4 tbsp plain flour

1 bunch spring onions (white part and 5cm (2in) of green), slivered

2 cloves garlic, finely chopped

30g (1oz) chopped fresh parsley

3 tbsp chopped fresh mint or 1½ tbsp chopped fresh marjoram

Salt and ground black pepper to taste

Quickly rinse the courgettes, then, using your hands or a tea towel, squeeze out the excess liquid. Add the courgettes to the batter. Preheat the oven to 95°C (200°F) Gas ½.

Heat in a large frying pan:

2 tbsp olive oil

Drop in the batter, using 4 tbsp for a 10cm (4in) cake. Fry over medium heat until golden brown on the bottom, about 4 minutes. Turn and brown the second side. Keep the fried pancakes warm in the oven while you fry the remaining batter, adding more oil if needed.

Sweetcorn Fritters

4 servings

Sweetcorn geneticists have engineered a bundle of sugar-enhanced and supersweet hybrids that are designed to remain sweet and nonstarchy while shipped and stored for supermarket sales. That is why we now get fresh supermarket sweetcorn all winter long. Compared to most summer corn, however, winter sweetcorn lacks moisture, creaminess, and tenderness.

Cut and scrape the kernels from:

5 ears sweetcorn

Place the sweetcorn and pulp in a large bowl and stir in:

2 large egg yolks, lightly beaten

2 tbsp plain flour

1 tbsp sugar

¼ tsp salt

⅛ tsp ground black pepper

Beat until the peaks are stiff but not dry:

2 large egg whites

Fold the egg whites into the sweetcorn mixture. Heat in a large nonstick frying pan over high heat until hot:

30g (1oz) butter or 2 tbsp vegetable oil

Drop in the batter, a heaped tbsp at a time. Reduce the heat to medium and cook until browned on the bottom, 2 to 3 minutes. Turn once (do not pat the fritters down) and cook the second side until browned. Take care not to overcook them. Serve immediately.

Potato and Aubergine Curry with Tomato and Fresh Coriander

4 servings

If you like, replace the aubergine with the same amount of courgettes.

Cut into 2cm (¾ in) dice:

1 large aubergine

Peel and cut into 1cm (½ in) dice:

3 medium boiling potatoes

Chop and reserve the juice from:

400g (14oz) tin whole tomatoes

Heat in a large cast-iron or other heavy frying pan over medium-high heat:

3 tbsp rapeseed oil

Add and stir-fry until lightly browned and fragrant, about 20 seconds:

1 tsp cumin seeds

Add and stir-fry for 30 more seconds:

½ tsp finely chopped garlic
½ tsp grated or finely chopped fresh ginger
¼ tsp turmeric

Add the tomatoes (without the juice) to the pan along with:

1 tsp sugar
½ tsp salt

Cook until most of the liquid is evaporated and the oil begins to separate and pool, about 3 minutes. Add the aubergine, potatoes and tomato juice. Cover and simmer until the vegetables are tender, about 20 minutes. Stir in:

2 tbsp fresh lemon juice
2 tbsp chopped fresh coriander
1 serrano or jalapeño pepper, finely chopped

Serve with:

Indian or pitta bread

Saag Paneer

4 servings

Saag Paneer, which literally translates as "spinach cheese", is a typical Indian vegetarian combination of vegetables and protein, in this case a fresh cheese. Our recipe is a variation on the traditional recipe – the spinach is stir-fried quickly rather than cooked to a purée. Be sure to use a nonstick pan to fry the cheese so it does not stick.

In a medium, heavy saucepan, bring to a boil:

1 litre (1½ pints) whole milk

Remove the pan from the heat and add:

3 tbsp fresh lemon juice

Stir until the milk curdles and separates into bits of solid curd floating in the liquid whey. Let stand for 5 minutes, then pour through a fine-mesh sieve lined with a double layer of muslin. Let stand until cool enough to handle, then pull the corners of the cloth together over the curd and squeeze out as much liquid as possible. Flatten the curd, still in the muslin, to a thickness of 1-2.5cm (½ -1in). Set it on a plate and top with another plate. Weigh down with a tin can and let stand for 20 minutes, then cut the cheese into 1cm (½ in) cubes.

Coarsely chop:

630g (1¼lb) spinach, stemmed and washed well

Heat in a large nonstick frying pan over medium-high heat:

60ml (2floz) rapeseed oil

Add and cook until lightly browned, about 15 seconds:

1 tsp cumin seeds

Add the cheese cubes and sauté, shaking the pan every now and then to turn the cubes, until golden brown, 3 to 4 minutes. Remove the cheese and set aside. Add to the oil in the pan:

1 medium onion, thinly sliced

Cook until softened and translucent, 3 to 4 minutes. Add and sauté for 1 minute:

4 cloves garlic, thinly sliced
2 small dried red chilli peppers

Add as much chopped spinach as will comfortably fit into the pan, cover and cook until wilted enough to add more spinach. Add a few more handfuls of spinach, cover and continue until all the spinach is wilted. Sprinkle with:

½ tsp salt

Cook, uncovered, until all the water is evaporated. Fold in the fried cheese, remove the red peppers and serve hot.

Curried Parsnips

4 to 6 servings

Serve as a main course over rice or lentils.

Peel, core and cut into large matchsticks (batons):

750g (1½lb) parsnips

Drop into a pot of boiling salted water and boil for 2 minutes; drain. Cook in a large frying pan over medium heat until softened, about 5 minutes:

45g (1½oz) butter or 3 tbsp vegetable oil

½ onion, finely diced

Add and cook, stirring constantly, for 1 minute:

1 tbsp curry powder

Stir in:

125ml (4floz) *Vegetable Stock, 17,* **or whole milk**

Add the parsnips and simmer, covered, over low heat until tender, about 10 minutes. Stir in but do not boil:

125g (4oz) yoghurt

Season with:

Salt and ground black pepper to taste

Garnish with:

4 slender spring onions (including 5cm/2in green), thinly sliced

Fresh coriander sprigs (optional)

Moroccan-Style Vegetable Stew

6 servings

Serve this wonderful stew over a bed of warm couscous.

Heat in a large flameproof casserole:

30g (1oz) butter or 2 tbsp olive oil

Add and cook over medium heat for 2 to 3 minutes:

2 medium onions, chopped

Stir in:

375ml (12floz) *Vegetable Stock, 17*

Simmer, stirring often, over medium-low heat until the onions are very tender, about 20 minutes.

Meanwhile, mix in a large bowl:

1 tsp ground cumin

¾ tsp chilli powder

½ tsp ground cardamom

½ tsp ground cinnamon

½ tsp freshly grated or ground nutmeg

Pinch of ground cloves

Stir in:

1 small butternut squash (750g/ 1½ lb), peeled, halved, seeded and cut into 1cm (½in) cubes

1 large baking potato (315g/ 10oz), peeled, halved and cut into 2cm (¾in) pieces

Add the squash mixture to the onions along with:

3 medium carrots, peeled and cut into 5mm (¼in) slices

4 tbsp raisins

5 cloves garlic, finely chopped

Bring to a simmer, then reduce the heat to medium-low. Cover first with a sheet of foil placed directly on the surface of the vegetables, then with the lid. Simmer gently

until the vegetables are completely tender, about 25 minutes.

Stir in:

1 or 2 medium courgettes, halved lengthwise, cut into 1cm (⅓in) slices

400g (14oz) tinned chickpeas, rinsed and drained

60g (2oz) halved stoned Kalamata or Niçoise olives

1 tsp salt ·

¼ tsp ground black pepper

Simmer, covered, until the courgette is tender, about 10 minutes. Stir in:

4 tbsp chopped fresh parsley or coriander

3 tbsp fresh lemon juice

Several drops of Tabasco sauce

Winter Root Vegetable Braise

4 main-dish servings

Serve this stew in soup plates with pieces of garlic-rubbed toast, or surround it with mashed potatoes. In addition to the vegetables listed, you could also include fennel, salsify, parsley root, artichokes and Jerusalem artichokes.

Heat in a large frying pan or flame-proof casserole over medium heat:

1½ tbsp olive oil
15g (½oz) butter
1 bay leaf
1 large sprig fresh thyme

Add:

2 onions, diced

Cook, stirring occasionally, until the onions begin to brown and have left a sugary residue on the bottom of the pan, about 12 minutes. Add and cook for 3 minutes more:

4 large mushrooms, wiped clean and thickly sliced
2 cloves garlic, finely chopped

Pour in:

125ml (4floz) dry white wine

Increase the heat and boil, scraping the bottom of the pan, until the liquid is reduced to a syrup, about 5 minutes. Add:

250g (8oz) turnips, peeled and quartered
250g (8oz) small swedes, peeled and cut into 2.5cm (1in) cubes
500g (1lb) celeriac, peeled and cut into 2.5cm (1in) cubes
1 tbsp plain flour
½ tsp salt

Stir the vegetables together, then pour in:

625ml (1 pint) *Vegetable Stock*, 17

Bring to a boil. Reduce the heat and simmer, covered, until the vegetables are tender, 20 to 25 minutes. Mix together:

3 tbsp double cream
1 tbsp Dijon mustard

Pour this into the stew and stir well. Season with:

Ground black pepper to taste
Fresh thyme leaves or chopped fresh parsley

Mushroom Ragout

4 servings

Serve over soft polenta, rice, garlic-rubbed croutons, or Yorkshire puddings. For more intense flavour, soak 15g (½ oz) dried mushrooms, chop and add with the fresh mushrooms; use the soaking water for part of the liquid.

Heat over medium-high heat in a large saucepan:

1 tbsp olive oil

Add and cook until golden, about 10 minutes:

1 onion, diced

Remove and set aside. Heat in the same pan over medium heat:

1 tbsp olive oil

Add and cook until they begin to release their liquid:

500g (1lb) assorted fresh mushrooms, wiped clean and thickly sliced

Add the onions along with:

2 cloves garlic, finely chopped
1 tsp chopped fresh rosemary, or scant ½ tsp dried
Salt and cracked black peppercorns to taste

Cook until the mushrooms begin to brown, another 3 to 4 minutes. Stir in:

1 tbsp tomato purée

Increase the heat to high and cook, stirring, for 1 to 2 minutes more. Add:

375ml (12floz) *Vegetable Stock*, 17

Reduce the heat and simmer for 10 minutes. Stir in to form a sauce:

30g (1oz) butter, cut into pieces
1½ tsp balsamic vinegar

Garnish with:

Grated Parmesan cheese (optional)
Chopped fresh parsley

MUSHROOMS

These days, you can find a variety of mushrooms at the supermarket. Porcini, also called cèpes or boletus, look like very large button mushrooms with thick stalks and reddish caps. They are among the tastiest of wild mushrooms. Chanterelles, or girolles, resemble a curving trumpet. Their golden or orange-brown caps and slender stems can hint of apricots or be delicately earthy. Chestnut are the same as common button mushrooms, only grown outdoors and bigger. Oyster mushrooms have small fan-shaped caps with short stems, cream coloured to greyish brown. Their texture is smooth, and their flavour can have a touch of the sea.

Greek Spinach and Cheese Pie (Spanakopita)

About thirty 5cm (2in) squares or diamonds

Stem, wash well, and coarsely chop:

1kg (2lb) spinach

Heat in a large frying pan over medium heat:

2 tbsp olive oil

Add and cook until softened, 5 to 7 minutes:

1 large onion, finely chopped
4 spring onions, finely chopped

Add the chopped spinach a handful at a time. Cook until the spinach is wilted and the liquid is released, 5 minutes. Increase the heat to high and cook, stirring often, until the liquid is evaporated and the spinach is dry, 7 to 10 minutes. Stir in:

4 tbsp snipped fresh dill or chopped fresh parsley

Let stand until cool enough to handle, then squeeze to remove the excess liquid. In a medium bowl, lightly beat:

4 large eggs

Add the cooked spinach mixture along with:

250g (8oz) feta cheese, crumbled
2 tbsp grated kefalotiri (Greek grating cheese) or Parmesan cheese
½ tsp salt
Several grinds of black pepper
Pinch of freshly grated or ground nutmeg

Lightly oil a 33 x 23cm (13 x 9in) baking tin. Melt:

125g (4oz) butter

Unroll on a dry work surface:

500g (1lb) filo pastry, thawed if frozen

Trim 2.5cm (1in) from the edges of the filo pastry. Cover with cling film and cover the cling film with a damp tea towel. Lay 1 sheet of filo in and up the sides of the prepared pan and brush lightly with melted butter. Top with 7 more filo sheets, brushing each one lightly with butter. Spread the spinach mixture over the layered filo. Top with 8 more sheets, brushing each one with butter, including the top sheet. Roll the overhanging filo from the sides to form a border all the way around. With a thin, sharp knife, cut the pie into squares or diamonds, but do not cut through the bottom or the filling will leak onto the pan. Refrigerate for 30 minutes. Preheat the oven to 190°C (375°F) Gas 5.

Bake the spinach pie until crisp and golden, about 45 minutes. Remove from the oven and let stand for a few minutes. Cut the squares or diamonds right through to the bottom and serve.

WORKING WITH FILO

Filo, from the word "leaf" in Greek, is available frozen in most supermarkets or fresh from some Greek and Middle Eastern bakeries. It is essential to keep the thin sheets from drying out. If using frozen filo, thaw it slowly, without unwrapping, in the refrigerator for several hours or overnight. Once it is thawed, unwrap the filo and remove only the number of sheets required for the recipe; rewrap the remaining sheets in cling film and return to the refrigerator or freezer.

Red Peppers Stuffed with Saffron Rice and Pine Nuts

4 to 6 servings

Halve lengthwise, keeping the stems intact, and seed:

2 large or 3 medium red peppers

Steam over boiling water until slightly softened, 8 to 10 minutes. Heat in a wide saucepan:

2 tbsp olive oil

Add and cook over medium heat until softened:

6 spring onions (white part and 2.5cm/1in green), chopped

3 cloves garlic, finely chopped

⅛ tsp crushed saffron threads

Add and stir briefly to coat with oil:

315g (10oz) long-grain white rice

Add and bring to a boil:

430ml (14floz) water or
Vegetable Stock, 17

Stir, reduce the heat to low, and cover. Cook for 10 minutes, then let stand, covered, for 10 minutes more. Preheat the oven to 180°C (350°F) Gas 4.

Fluff the rice, turn it into a large bowl to cool, then add:

185g (6oz) grated provolone cheese

45g (1½ oz) pine nuts, toasted

4 tbsp chopped fresh parsley

2 tbsp chopped fresh marjoram or basil

Mix well and season with:

Salt and ground black pepper to taste

Place the peppers in a baking dish in which they fit snugly. Spoon the filling into each pepper half, mounding the top. Add to the bottom of the dish:

125ml (4floz) water

Cover lightly with foil and bake until heated through, about 35 minutes. Serve sprinkled with:

Chopped fresh parsley

Summer Squash Gratin

6 servings

This crumbly, golden gratin is irresistible. Try it with pattypan or straightneck squash. Pattypan or scallop squash are flattened rounds with scalloped edges, picked 7.5cm (3in) wide or less. Their flavour is lighter and nuttier than courgette. Heritage pattypans are pale green. Hybrids are more rounded and can be gold or dark green. Straightneck squash have the same flavour as pattypan but look like yellow courgettes.

Preheat the oven to 180°C (350°F) Gas 4. Lightly butter a 25cm (10in) gratin dish.

Steam until tender, about 10 minutes:

625g (1¼ lb) yellow squash, cut into 1cm (½ in) cubes

Remove to a medium bowl. Cook in  a small frying pan until softened:

15g (½oz) butter or 1 tbsp olive oil

½ small onion, finely diced

Add to the squash along with:

60g (2oz) diced Gruyère, raclette, Swiss or Teleme cheese

5 tbsp crème fraîche

2 tbsp grated Parmesan cheese

1 tbsp white vermouth or dry white wine

1 tsp ground coriander

Salt and ground white pepper to taste

Pour into the prepared dish. Combine and sprinkle over the top:

45g (1½oz) fresh breadcrumbs

15g (½oz) butter, melted

Bake until bubbling and golden, about 35 minutes.

Kale and Potato Gratin

6 servings

Kale deserves to be appreciated as much as spinach. Its crisp, curled, crinkly or deeply cut leaves have a rich but delicate cabbage taste and hold their texture in cooking.

Preheat the oven to 180°C (350°F) Gas 4. Butter a 2 litre (3¼ pint) gratin dish. Have ready:

4 medium baking potatoes (about 625g/1¼ lb), peeled and cut into 2mm (⅛in) thick rounds

2 small onions, cut into 2mm (⅛in) thick slices

Steam until almost tender, 8 to 10 minutes:

1 large bunch (about 500g/1lb) kale, stemmed and washed

Drain and let stand until cool enough to handle. Press out the excess water and coarsely chop. In the gratin dish, build up alternating layers of potatoes, onions and kale, beginning and ending with the potatoes. Dot each onion layer with:

15g (½oz) butter, cut into pieces

½ tsp finely chopped fresh tarragon

¼ tsp salt

⅛ tsp ground black pepper

Pour over the layers:

375ml (12floz) milk or single cream

Cover and bake until the potatoes are tender and almost all the liquid is absorbed, 30 to 45 minutes. Grill, if desired, to brown the top. Serve.

Rolled Stuffed Aubergine

4 servings

A great summer main course. The rolls can be formed well in advance and refrigerated before baking.

Preheat the oven to 200°C (400°F) Gas 6. Lightly oil a 33 x 23cm (13 x 9in) baking dish.

Combine in a bowl:

90g (3oz) grated provolone or mozzarella cheese

220g (7oz) ricotta cheese

2 tbsp grated Parmesan cheese

2 tbsp chopped fresh marjoram or basil

1 small clove garlic, finely chopped

Cut lengthwise into 5mm (¼in) thick slices:

1 large aubergine (about 625g/ 1¼ lb)

Brush both sides of the slices with:

Olive oil

Cook the aubergine in batches in a frying pan until golden, about

5 minutes each side, then remove to a platter. Spread a mound of the cheese mixture at the base of each aubergine slice, then roll it up. Arrange the rolls seam side down in the baking dish. Cover the dish and bake until heated through and the cheese is melted, about 20 minutes. Remove the rolls to warmed plates. Serve surrounded with:

Italian Tomato Sauce, 46

Vegetable Pie with Cheddar Scone Crust

8 to 12 servings

This dish can be prepared up to 1 day ahead: cut up, brown and place the vegetables in the baking dish. The crust can be made up to 2 hours ahead and kept covered at room temperature. Keep the vegetables in large chunks so that they remain intact and do not cook down to a purée.

Prepare and keep each vegetable in separate bowls:

2 medium red onions (about 500g/1lb), cut into thick slices
3 medium carrots, peeled and cut into 2.5cm (1in) pieces
3 parsnips, peeled and cut into 2.5cm (1in) pieces
1 celeriac, peeled and cut into 2.5cm (1in) pieces
1 butternut squash (about 1.25kg/ 2½ lb), peeled and cut into 2.5cm (1in) pieces
1 acorn squash (about 750g/ 1½ lb), peeled and cut into 2.5cm (1in) pieces
250g (8oz) portobello mushrooms, cut into thick slices and slices halved crosswise

Have ready:

3 or 4 tbsp olive oil
45-60g (1½ -2oz) unsalted butter

Heat ½ tbsp oil and 10g (¼ oz) butter in a large frying pan over medium-high heat. Add the onion slices and cook until browned, about 3 minutes on each side. Transfer to a large bowl and season with:

Salt and ground black pepper

Add a bit more oil and butter to the pan, then add the carrots and parsnips. Brown, stirring frequently, for 5 to 7 minutes, transfer to the bowl, and season with salt and pepper. Repeat, adding oil and butter as needed, with the celeriac

and squashes, browning them all separately and seasoning with salt and pepper as you place them in the bowl. Finally, add the mushrooms to the pan with more oil and butter if needed, turn the heat to high, and brown them well, tossing frequently, about 5 to 7 minutes. Add to the bowl and season with salt and pepper. Preheat the oven to 200°C (400°F) Gas 6. Add to the vegetables:

2 tbsp chopped fresh marjoram, or 1 tbsp dried

Gently mix the herb and vegetables together, transfer to a 33 x 23cm (13 x 9in) baking dish, and spread evenly in 1 layer. Pour over the vegetables:

1 litre (1½ pints) *Vegetable Stock*, 17

Cover the dish and bake until the vegetables are just tender when pierced with the tip of a sharp knife, 30 to 45 minutes. While the vegetables bake, prepare the cheese crust. Whisk together thoroughly in a large bowl:

315g (10oz) plain flour
2½ tsp baking powder
½ to ¾ tsp salt

Drop in:

75-90g (2½-3oz) cold unsalted butter, cut into pieces

Cut in the butter with 2 knives or a pastry blender, tossing the pieces with the flour mixture to coat and separate them as you work. For scones with crunchy edges and a flaky, layered structure, continue to cut in the butter until the largest pieces are the size of peas and the rest resemble breadcrumbs. For classic fluffy scones, continue to cut in the butter until the mixture resembles coarse breadcrumbs. Do

not allow the butter to melt or form a paste with the flour.

Add all at once:

180ml (6floz) double cream
75g (2½ oz) grated Cheddar cheese
2 tsp finely chopped garlic (optional)
¼ tsp cracked black pepper

Mix with a rubber spatula, wooden spoon or fork just until most of the dry ingredients are moistened. With a lightly floured hand, gather the dough into a ball and knead it gently against the sides and bottom of the bowl 5 to 10 times, turning and pressing any loose pieces into the dough each time until they adhere and the bowl is fairly clean. Set aside. After the vegetables have cooked for 30 to 45 minutes, uncover the dish and spoon dollops of scone dough over the vegetables. Continue baking until the scones are browned, 20 to 25 minutes more. Remove from the oven, let stand for 10 minutes, and serve.

CELERIAC

More or less round, it has a daunting appearance – knobby, grimy and perhaps tangled at the roots. But beneath the skin is tender, cream-coloured flesh with a nutty taste. An autumn and winter vegetable, it is also called celery root and turnip-root celery. Select small to medium knobs, heavy for their size. They should have no cuts, bruises or soft spots. If there are stalks on top, they should be crisp and fresh. You can use the stalks for seasoning – they have the concentrated flavour of Chinese celery.

Tuscan-Style Stuffed Artichokes

6 appetizer servings

Preheat the oven to 190°C (375°F) Gas 5. Trim as directed below:

6 medium artichokes

To prevent discolouration, rub all the cut surfaces with:

½ lemon

Combine well:

6 tbsp extra-virgin olive oil
6 tbsp fresh breadcrumbs, toasted
4 tbsp chopped fresh parsley

3 cloves garlic, finely chopped
3 tbsp grated Parmesan cheese
Salt and ground black pepper
  to taste

Using a teaspoon, fill the cavities of the artichokes with this mixture. Place the stuffed artichokes in a baking dish in which they fit snugly. Pour 1cm (½ in) of water into the bottom of the dish and add to it:

Juice of ½ lemon
1 tbsp extra-virgin olive oil

Cover the dish with foil and bake until the artichokes are tender, about 45 minutes. Serve warm or at room temperature.

HOW TO PREPARE ARTICHOKES

Have on hand a lemon half or two; its juice rubbed over cut surfaces keeps the flesh from discolouring.

1 Use scissors to trim off the tough, thorny tops of the outside layers of leaves. Bend each leaf back and snap off the top, or snip it off with scissors – the only method that works with tough end-of-the-season artichokes. Rub cut surfaces frequently with lemon.

2 When you reach the thin inner leaves that are green at the top but celery yellow at the base, lay the artichokes on their sides on a chopping board. With a sharp, heavy, stainless-steel knife or a serrated knife, trim off the top 2.5cm (1in) or so of the inner leaves.

3 Pull out the immature prickly, pinkish leaves in the centre.

4 Use the tip of a spoon to scrape up the thicket of fuzz beneath, called the choke. It will lift up in small pieces. Be careful not to cut into the heart.

Garlic-Braised Sprouting Broccoli or Rapini

4 servings

Sprouting broccoli's leaves and buds are mustardy but sweet; it is a purplish autumn green. Rapini, a springtime green, is another mostly leafy plant and is often confused with sprouting broccoli. Rapini leaves and buds have a mustardy bite, much like turnip greens, which they resemble.

Bring to a rolling boil in a stockpot:

4 litres (6½ pints) water
1½ tbsp salt

Thinly slice the greens, peel the stems, and cut into 2.5cm (1in) pieces:

1 bunch sprouting broccoli or rapini (about 500g/1lb)

Boil for 2 minutes, then drain and squeeze the moisture out of the leaves. Heat in a large frying pan over medium heat:

2 tbsp extra-virgin olive oil

Add:

1 clove garlic, thinly sliced
1 small dried red chilli pepper (optional)

Add the broccoli and cook over medium heat until tender, about 4 minutes. Remove the chilli pepper and season with:

Salt and ground black pepper to taste

Serve hot.

June Vegetable Ragout

4 servings

You can substitute packets of frozen artichoke hearts, thawed and quartered, for the fresh artichokes in this recipe. It is worth it, though, to make this dish with fresh artichokes.

Trim and quarter:

8 large artichoke hearts, or 16 baby artichokes

As you work, drop them into a bowl of water with lemon juice added. Cut lengthwise in half and peel:

2 medium onions

Place each half, cut side down, on a chopping board and cut crosswise into very thin slices. In an unheated large frying pan, combine the onions with:

6 tbsp extra-virgin olive oil
1 plump head garlic, separated into cloves and peeled, cloves halved lengthwise
1 small bunch summer savory or stems and sprigs of thyme and parsley, tied with kitchen string
Salt to taste

Toss to coat the ingredients with the oil. Cover and sweat over low heat until the onions are softened, about 10 minutes. Drain and add the artichokes and:

1kg (2lb) broad beans, blanched, refreshed and shelled
3 tomatoes, peeled, seeded and coarsely chopped

375ml (12floz) dry white wine

Simmer, uncovered, for 10 minutes to evaporate the alcohol. Add:

1kg (2lb) fresh peas in their pods, shelled, blanched and refreshed
20 asparagus tips, blanched and refreshed

Cook until the green vegetables are heated through, about 2 minutes more. Remove the pan from the heat and immediately stir in until creamy:

30g (1oz) cold unsalted butter, cut into small pieces

Remove and discard the bundle of herbs. Taste for seasoning. Serve immediately with crusty bread.

ABOUT
BEANS
& TOFU

*A*n excellent source of protein, vitamins, minerals and fibre, beans are what nutritionists like to call a "powerhouse" – a food that is unusually rich in nutrients but relatively low in calories. Because they are digested slowly, and thus raise blood sugar very gently, they are sometimes recommended for diabetics. Their high fibre content, both water soluble and nonsoluble, has been linked to lower blood cholesterol. And it is suspected that beans contain some compounds that protect against cancers.

Tofu is the humble soybean's leap toward culinary art, especially in the cuisines of China, where it was invented more than a thousand years ago, and Japan. Tofu (also called bean curd and dofu) is made like cheese, by coagulating soy milk until it forms curds, which are broken up and then pressed. But tofu is unlike cheese in that it rarely stands on its own. Instead, it bathes in the flavours of sauces, marinades and dressings. Its smoothness can range from as soft as custard to as chewy as a bread dumpling. A 125g (4oz) serving provides up to one-quarter of a day's protein requirement, about 10 grams of fat and no cholesterol. Since most tofu is coagulated with a calcium compound, it also provides a goodly amount of that mineral.

Red Bean and Lima Succotash, 82

Soaking and Cooking Beans

Whether or not to soak beans before cooking is a hot topic today. Many noted food professionals, whose opinions we hold in high regard, argue that fresh dried beans do not benefit from presoaking before cooking. Heating the pulses to boiling and then simmering them until they swell with water and soften can be done in one continuous process. In order to ensure success with this method, the beans must be of high quality and fresh. Given the limited availability of high-quality fresh beans, presoaking the beans first is kinder, both to the bean and to the cook. Not only does it save anywhere from 30 minutes to over an hour on the stove, but it also treats the seed coat more gently than steady simmering, so that the shape of the bean holds without breaking. At high elevations, where simmering times will be extended by the lower temperature of the boiling water, soaking for up to 24 hours is good time-saving insurance.

Before you prepare any pulses, spread them in a pan or large colander and remove any tiny stones that may have accompanied them out of the field. Then rinse the beans very well under cold water, raking them with your fingers to get rid of any clumps of dirt.

Our preferred soaking method is to heat the soaking water, which hastens the swelling of the beans. For a gentle quick-soak, pour boiling water over the beans to cover by 5cm (2in), cover, let stand until the beans have swelled to at least twice their size and have absorbed most of the water and then drain, discarding the soaking liquid. This will take at least an hour and possibly longer, but the beans will remain firm and keep their shape when cooked.

Another way to soak beans is to place them in a large bowl or pot and add water to cover by at least 5cm (2in). Cover and let stand for up to 24 hours; refrigerate to prevent fermentation if the kitchen

is very warm. The beans will swell to triple their dried size. Drain well and discard the soaking liquid.

A third method, which risks breaking some bean skins, is to place the beans in a saucepan, add water to cover by 5cm (2in), and heat to boiling; then reduce the heat and simmer for 2 minutes. Let stand, covered, for 1 hour. Or microwave 500g (1lb) beans and 1 litre (1½ pints) water in a covered 3-4 litre (5-6 pint) casserole on high to boiling, 12 to 17 minutes, and then on medium for 2 minutes. Stir and let stand, covered, for 1 hour. With all three soaking methods, be sure to rinse and drain the beans before the final cooking.

To cook, place beans in a large pot and add cold water to cover by 5cm (2in). Bring to a boil over high heat; skim off the foam that rises to the surface. Reduce the heat to low and cover; simmer, stirring and skimming occasionally, until the beans are tender. Do not boil rapidly or the abrasion will loosen the bean skins. If the pot threatens to boil over, partially remove the cover.

Beans readily absorb seasonings from water. Simmer beans with chopped onions and carrots to sweeten them; use at least 125g (4oz) of each with 500g (1lb) of beans, because the water will dilute their impact.

If you want relatively firm beans, for a salad or side dish, remove a few beans and pinch them for tenderness at the low end of the cooking time range suggested in the recipe. If you want very soft beans for a soup, you may decide to cook them longer than suggested.

SUBSTITUTING TINNED BEANS

Tinned beans can be substituted in recipes that call for cooked beans, but they are almost always softer and less flavourful. Since brands vary in quality, it is worth trying different ones. When choosing tinned beans, certain varieties hold up better during the canning process than others. White beans seem to stand up less well to canning than, for example, chickpeas. Rinsing tinned beans improves the taste a little and removes excess salt.

HOW TO SPROUT BEANS

To make 90g (3oz) sprouts, start with 3 tbsp dried beans. Seeds, such as alfalfa, wheat and radish, can be sprouted the same way.

1 Pick over and rinse beans. Place in a large bowl and cover with about 5cm (2in) warm (not hot) water. Let stand for up to 24 hours; drain and rinse.

2 Place the beans in a sterile 1-litre (1½ pint) glass jar. Cover with a double layer of muslin (or a finer-weave cloth if sprouting very small seeds) and secure with a rubber band.

3 Twice a day, fill the jar with cool water and drain it off through the muslin. Be sure to drain well to avoid inviting mould.

4 Pale shoots should appear within 5 days and are ready to harvest when about 2.5cm (1in) long. Before harvesting, place the jar in the sun for a few hours to encourage the shoots to produce chlorophyll. Discard beans that do not sprout.

Sprouting Beans

The most fundamental bean transformation is sprouting, or turning the bean and its embryo into the beginnings of a plant. Almost all organically grown beans, if not too old, can be sprouted, but do not sprout broad beans, for there may be some risk in eating these raw. Lentils and adzuki and mung beans, those that make the threadlike sprouts commonly used in Chinese cooking, are good choices, because small beans tend to sprout more readily than large ones. Small amounts of sprouts can be eaten raw – in a sandwich or sprinkled over a salad, for example – but if you are using more than a large handful, heat them briefly to improve digestibility. You can add them towards the end of cooking to other vegetables, grains and stir-fries.

The vivid variety of sprouted pulses available – more bean than sprout in most cases – make good snacks and salad ingredients. They also contribute texture and colour to rice; add them, without stirring, for the last few minutes of cooking.

Tofu

Tofu is as perishable as dairy foods and highly susceptible to bacterial contamination, so wash your hands and work surfaces and keep the tofu refrigerated as you would milk and cheese. When buying refrigerated tofu, check the expiry date. You can leave it in its tub or pouch, but it is better to open the package, discard the liquid and pour in fresh water; change the water daily. It will keep this way for up to a week, depending on its freshness when purchased. Because of the risk of contamination, it is best to avoid tofu sold from open tubs, even if it is refrigerated.

The tofu called "silken", often sold in aseptic boxes, is labelled soft or firm, but either one is much more fragile than regular tofu. Made more like yoghurt than like cheese, silken tofu is coagulated from thick soy milk and not pressed.

The tofu used for cooking, sometimes called "cotton" tofu, is labelled soft, firm or extra firm, depending on how much liquid was drained off during processing. Firm and extra firm hold together better in the pot. Cooks commonly firm up tofu by pressing it under a weight for 30 to 60 minutes, depending on how much water the tofu starts out with and the desired firmness.

HOW TO PRESS TOFU

1 For a 500g (1lb) block of tofu, cut it horizontally in half to make two slabs, each about 2.5cm (1in) thick.

2 Place a sheet of foil over a chopping board large enough to hold both slabs side by side. To allow the water to drain off, place one end of the board over the edge of the sink or on a baking tray and prop up the other end with a small cup measure or a 2.5cm (1in) thick box.

3 Place the tofu on the board and cover with another sheet of foil. Place a second chopping board or similarly shaped weight over the tofu and let stand for 10 minutes to compact somewhat. The sides of the tofu should bulge very slightly, but be careful not to overweight soft tofu before it has compacted, or it may split. After 10 minutes, add more weight, evenly distributed; a cast-iron frying pan or casserole with two or three large tin cans in it, several nested heavy frying pans, or several large books will do the job. Check the weighted tofu for firmness after 30 minutes; if desired, turn the slabs over, replace the weight, and press for an additional 15 to 30 minutes. Refrigerate pressed tofu in a bowl of water; it will not reabsorb water and can be kept for 2 to 3 days if you change the water daily. This extra step is not essential, just a textural refinement.

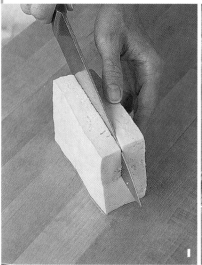

Classic Black Beans (Frijoles Negros)

6 servings

These are delicious served with nothing more than a spoonful of sour cream or yoghurt and some diced avocados, but they are also very good served in warm tortillas or as a soup garnished with coriander leaves. Pinto, pink, kidney and navy beans can be substituted for the black beans.

Pick over and rinse:

500g (1lb) dried black beans

Drain. Heat in a large saucepan over medium heat:

3 tbsp vegetable oil

Add:

1 medium onion, diced

Cook, stirring often, until deep golden brown, about 10 minutes. Stir in the beans along with:

2 litres (3¼ pints) water

1 large sprig fresh epazote (optional)

1 fresh jalapeño pepper or dried chipotle pepper, halved and seeded (optional)

Remove any beans that float. Bring to a boil. Reduce the heat to medium-low and simmer, partially covered, until the beans are thoroughly tender, about 1 hour. Stir the beans regularly and add water as needed to keep the liquid a generous 1cm (½ in) above the level of the beans.

Season with:

Salt and ground black pepper to taste

Simmer for another 10 to 15 minutes for the beans to absorb the seasoning, then remove from the heat. Serve hot.

Refried Beans

6 servings

A classic Mexican side dish.

Heat in a large frying pan over medium-high heat:

2 tbsp vegetable oil

Add:

1 medium white onion, chopped

Cook, stirring often, until deep golden brown, about 10 minutes. Add:

4 cloves garlic, finely chopped

Cook, stirring, for 1 minute.

Add with a slotted spoon a large spoonful at a time:

880g (28oz) undrained *Classic Black Beans, above,* or cooked black beans, undrained if tinned

Mash each addition of beans to a

coarse purée with a potato masher or the back of a large spoon before adding the next spoonful. Stir in:

250ml (8floz) cooking liquid or water

Cook, stirring often, over medium to low heat until the beans are a little soupier than you would like to serve them – they will thicken as they sit. The whole mashing and cooking process will take 10 to 15 minutes.

Season with:

Salt to taste

Serve warm with:

Crumbled queso fresco, feta or grated Parmesan cheese

Tortilla chips

Vegetarian Chilli

8 servings

A delicious "warmer upper" (opposite). Heat in a large saucepan over medium heat:

2 tbsp olive oil

Add:

125g (4oz) chopped peeled carrots
155g (5oz) chopped red peppers
155g (5oz) chopped green peppers
125g (4oz) chopped onions
2 cloves garlic, finely chopped

Cook, stirring, until the onions are golden, 12 to 15 minutes. Add:

1-2 fresh green chilli peppers,
  seeded and finely chopped, or
  1 chipotle pepper in adobo
  sauce, finely chopped
1 tbsp ground ancho chilli pepper
1 tbsp ground cumin

Cook, stirring, for 2 minutes. Stir in:

Two 400g (14oz) tins
  plum tomatoes, with juice,
  coarsely chopped

500g (16oz) tinned red kidney
  beans, rinsed and drained, or
  280g (9oz) cooked
500g (16oz) tinned cannellini
  beans, rinsed and drained, or
  280g (9oz) cooked
500g (16oz) tinned black beans,
  rinsed and drained, or 280g
  (9oz) cooked
250ml (8floz) tomato juice
Salt to taste

Bring to a boil. Reduce the heat to medium-low and simmer, uncovered, stirring occasionally, until the flavours are blended, adding more tomato juice or water as needed, about 45 minutes. Season and serve with:

Sour cream
Salsa Fresca, right
Chopped fresh coriander

Red Bean and Lima Succotash

4 servings

The most popular form of succotash combines sweetcorn with lima beans — but red kidney beans work too.
Pick over, rinse, and soak, 78:

90g (3oz) dried red kidney beans

Drain. Combine in a medium saucepan with water to cover by 5cm (2in). Bring to a boil. Reduce the heat and simmer, covered, until the beans are very tender, about 1½ hours. Add water as needed to keep the beans moist. Drain. Bring to a boil in a large saucepan:

250ml (8floz) double cream

Boil over medium heat until reduced to about 125ml (4floz),

being careful not to let it overflow. Add the cooked beans along with:

280g (9oz) fresh, tinned or frozen
  sweetcorn kernels
125g (4oz) cooked fresh or frozen
  baby lima beans

Cover and cook over low heat for 10 minutes. Stir in:

15g (½ oz) butter
1 tsp fresh thyme leaves (optional)
½ tsp salt
⅛ tsp ground black pepper

Taste and adjust the seasonings. Serve hot.

Salsa Fresca

About 500ml (16floz)

This recipe for Mexican salsa is easily doubled or tripled, but try to make only as much as you will use immediately, as it loses its texture on standing and the chilli peppers increase in heat. Regional variations include using spring onions or white or red onions, water instead of lime juice, and in Yucatán, sour-orange juice instead of lime juice. Any sort of fresh chilli pepper can be used. Rinsing the chopped onions eliminates the biting aftertaste that could otherwise overwhelm the other ingredients.

Combine in a medium bowl:

½ small white or red onion or
  8 slender spring onions, finely
  chopped, rinsed and drained
2 tbsp fresh lime juice or cold
  water

Prepare the following ingredients, setting them aside, then add all together to the onion mixture:

2 large ripe tomatoes, or 3-5
  ripe plum tomatoes, seeded, if
  desired, and finely diced
15-30g (½-1oz) chopped fresh
  coriander (leaves and tender
  stems)
3-5 serrano or fresh jalapeño
  peppers, or ¼-1 habanero
  pepper, or to taste, seeded and
  finely chopped
6 radishes, finely diced (optional)
1 medium clove garlic, finely
  chopped (optional)

Stir together well. Season with:

¼ tsp salt, or to taste

Serve immediately.

Couscous with Chickpeas

4 servings

Heat in a large frying pan over medium heat:

3 tbsp olive oil

Add:

125g (4oz) sliced blanched almonds

Cook, stirring, just until lightly golden, 2 to 3 minutes. Add:

3 cloves garlic, finely chopped

Cook, stirring, for about 1 minute. Stir in:

1 tsp sweet or hot paprika
1 tsp ground cumin
1 tsp ground coriander
½ to 1 tsp Tabasco sauce

Cook until heated through, about 1 minute more. Stir in:

625ml (1 pint) *Vegetable Stock, 17,* **or water**
375g (12oz) cooked chickpeas, rinsed and drained if tinned
185g (6oz) chopped raisins

Bring to a boil and stir in:

250g (8oz) quick-cooking couscous

Cover, remove from the heat and let stand for 5 minutes. Fluff the couscous with a fork. Season with:

Salt and ground black pepper to taste

Garnish with:

4 tbsp chopped fresh parsley or coriander

Curried Chickpeas with Vegetables

4 servings

This makes a perfect main course.

Heat in a large frying pan over medium heat until sizzling:

60ml (2floz) vegetable oil
2 tsp cumin seeds

Add:

1 tbsp chopped peeled fresh ginger
1 tbsp finely chopped garlic

Cook, stirring, over low heat for 1 minute; do not brown. Stir in:

2 tsp curry powder

Cook for 1 minute. Stir in:

315g (10oz) cooked chickpeas, rinsed and drained if tinned
500g (1lb) peeled sweet potatoes, cut into 1cm (½ in) cubes
250g (8oz) cauliflower florets

90g (3oz) green beans, cut into 2.cm (1in) pieces
250ml (8floz) *Vegetable Stock, 17*
½ to 1 tsp salt
Ground black pepper to taste

Cover and cook over medium heat until the vegetables are tender, about 10 minutes. Stir together:

250g (8oz) natural yoghurt
2 tbsp plain flour

Add to the vegetables along with:

1 tbsp finely chopped fresh jalapeño peppers

Cook, stirring, over low heat until heated through; do not boil. Toast in another frying pan over medium-low heat:

2 tbsp grated dried coconut, preferably unsweetened

Sprinkle over the vegetables. Top with:

4 tbsp chopped roasted unsalted cashews or peanuts

CHICKPEAS

Chickpeas seem indestructible. They come out of a tin firmer than other beans, hold up well in stews and salads, and can withstand grinding to make *Falafel, 44,* or baking for a pop-in-your-mouth snack. They are also known as garbanzos and ceci beans; a smaller variety is sold skinless and split as *chana dal* in Indian groceries and can be used instead of split peas to make *Dal, opposite.* Chickpeas are a constant in Mediterranean cuisines, from Middle Eastern hummus to Moroccan couscous, imparting a mild nutty flavour to all.

Classic Tuscan Beans

6 to 8 servings

Tuscans love beans so much that the rest of Italy calls them mangia fagioli, *"the bean eaters". Tradition and goodness come together in this simplest of cooking methods — simmering dried beans seasoned with fresh sage, garlic, and olive oil. Dried cannellini beans are a first choice for their sweet, creamy character. Haricot or pinto beans are a good alternative. Serve hot or at room temperature, drizzling on a thread of olive oil at the table.*

Pick over, rinse, and soak, 78:

500g (1lb) dried cannellini, haricot or pinto beans

Drain. Combine in a large pot with:

12 fresh sage leaves or whole dried sage leaves

3 cloves garlic, halved

1 tbsp extra-virgin olive oil

Add water to cover by 7.5cm (3in). Bring to a simmer, partially cover, and simmer gently until tender, about 1 hour. Drain. Season to taste with:

Salt and ground black pepper

Serve hot, warm or at room temperature, seasoning each portion with about:

1 tsp extra-virgin olive oil, preferably Tuscan

Indian Lentil Purée (Dal)

4 to 6 servings

Dal is the Hindi word for both an array of pulses used in Indian cooking and a preparation of pulses that is a staple of Indian cuisine. In Indian households where meat is either too expensive or prohibited by religion, dal is likely to be on the table at every meal as the protein. If the dal is puréed, it is soupy or "wet" and eaten with rice; if not puréed, the dal is "dry" and eaten with bread. A puréed dal may be thick or thin, as the cook chooses.

Pick over, rinse, and place in a large saucepan:

185g (6oz) yellow split peas or red lentils

Add:

500ml (16floz) water

1 small onion, sliced

¾ tsp finely chopped garlic

¾ tsp chopped peeled fresh ginger

½ tsp ground turmeric

Simmer, covered, until the split peas are tender, 20 to 25 minutes. Purée through a food mill and return to the saucepan. Stir in:

250ml (8floz) water

¾ tsp salt

Simmer, partially covered, until the dal is thickened to the consistency of split pea soup, about 20 minutes. Stir in:

2 fresh serrano or jalapeño peppers, seeded and cut into thirds

1 plum tomato, diced

2 tbsp chopped fresh coriander

Serve with:

Hot cooked rice

LENTILS

Whole lentils are thin skinned, require no soaking, and cook relatively quickly. The olive-coloured lentils sold everywhere are sometimes called green, other times brown, and are actually shades of both. French lentils (Puy are the finest example) are about half the size of the more common lentils, are a more grey-green, and have a deeper flavour. Italian lentils (Castelluccio being the best) are small, round, brown and deeply flavoured; they hold their shape when cooked, and offer a novel appearance. More colourful and very quick cooking are red and yellow lentils; both are skinless and, whether whole or split, dissolve into a purée as they cook.

Sesame Stir-Fried Lentils and Vegetables

4 to 6 servings

Lentils are used in this recipe much as plain cooked rice would be used in fried rice or in a frying pan dish of rice heated with vegetables. Serve over rice for a main course.

Toast in a small frying pan over medium heat for about 1 minute:

1 tbsp sesame seeds

Place in a vegetable steaming basket over boiling water:

185g (6oz) diagonally sliced peeled carrots

155g (5oz) broccoli florets

155g (5oz) halved pattypan squash

90g (3oz) trimmed snow peas

Cover and steam until crisp-tender, about 5 minutes. Rinse with cool water to stop the cooking. Heat in a large frying pan over medium-high heat:

2 tbsp vegetable oil

Add:

75g (2½ oz) red peppers, cut into 1cm (½ in) pieces

Cook, stirring, for about 2 minutes. Add:

1 tbsp finely chopped garlic

1 tbsp chopped peeled fresh ginger

¼ tsp crushed chilli flakes

Cook, stirring, until sizzling, about 30 seconds. Add the steamed vegetables along with:

250g (8oz) cooked brown or green lentils

90g (3oz) thinly sliced spring onions

3 tbsp light or dark soy sauce

2 tsp toasted sesame oil

Cook, stirring, just until heated through, about 3 minutes. Sprinkle with the toasted sesame seeds. Serve hot.

Szechuan Spiced Tofu

4 servings

Vary the hotness of this dish by adjusting the amount of chilli paste. As with all stir-fries, have all the ingredients measured, chopped and ready before beginning to cook.

Heat in a wok or large frying pan over medium-high heat:

1 tbsp peanut or vegetable oil

Add:

2 tsp chopped peeled fresh ginger
1 tsp finely chopped garlic

Stir-fry for 1 minute. Add:

250g (8oz) baby sweetcorn
375g (12oz) bok choy, cut into
1cm (½ in) slices
½ small onion, sliced

Stir-fry until the bok choy is slightly wilted, 3 to 4 minutes. Combine and stir in:

125ml (4floz) *Vegetable Stock,* **17**
2 tbsp light or dark soy sauce
1 tbsp black bean sauce or black
bean paste

1 tbsp dry sherry
2 tsp chilli paste
1 tbsp cornflour
½ tsp sugar
¼ tsp Szechuan peppercorns,
lightly cracked if desired

Boil, stirring, until thickened, about 1 minute. Stir in:

315g (10½oz) extra-firm tofu,
pressed if desired, 80, and cubed

Heat through for 2 to 3 minutes. Arrange on a serving platter:

375g (12oz) Chinese-style egg
noodles, cooked

Spoon the tofu mixture over the noodles and garnish with:

30g (1oz) grated peeled carrots
2 tbsp sliced spring onions

SZECHUAN PEPPERCORNS

The dried reddish-brown berries known as Szechuan peppercorns are not related to black peppercorns or chilli peppers. The spice has a clean, spicy-woodsy fragrance that has made it popular in all regions of China for centuries. Szechuan peppercorns are sold in plastic packets. They keep well in a covered jar.

Toast Szechuan peppercorns in a dry frying pan over medium heat until they begin to smoke (do not worry if a few blacken slightly) and then grind them in a mortar or spice grinder. Store excess powder in a jar. "Seasoned oil" – made by heating Szechuan peppercorns in peanut oil until they blacken, then straining the oil and discarding the peppercorns – makes a wonderful cooking oil for stir-fried dishes, or it may be used for dressing Chinese salads.

Smoked Tofu Burgers

6 servings

Tofu burgers are great for lunch or dinner. This flavourful mixture can also be baked as a loaf in a small loaf tin at 180°C (350°F) Gas 4 for 40 to 45 minutes.

Soak in warm water to cover until softened, about 20 minutes:

15g (½ oz) dried shiitake
mushrooms

Drain, discarding the liquid, and squeeze out the excess water from the mushrooms. Chop the mushrooms, discarding the tough centres and stems. Heat in a large

frying pan over medium heat:

2-3 tsp chilli sesame oil

Add the shiitakes along with:

125g (4oz) finely chopped
broccoli florets and stems
60g (2oz) finely chopped red peppers
4 tbsp sliced spring onions
2 tsp finely chopped peeled fresh
ginger
1½ tsp finely chopped garlic

Cook, stirring, until tender, 4 to 5 minutes. Combine with:

185g (6oz) smoked tofu, finely
chopped

220g (7oz) cooked brown rice
60g (2oz) dry breadcrumbs
2 large eggs, lightly beaten
1 tbsp light or dark soy sauce

Remove to a food processor and pulse several times, until a spoonful of the mixture can be pressed into a ball. Shape the mixture into 6 patties (or burgers). Cook in a lightly greased frying pan over medium heat until browned, 3 to 5 minutes each side. Serve hot on rolls.

Moo Shu Tempeh

12 pancakes; 6 servings

If cooking time does not allow this pancake preparation, warm flour tortillas will substitute nicely.

Stir together until crumbly:

80ml (3floz) boiling water

155g (5oz) plain flour

Shape into a ball and knead on a lightly floured surface until the dough is very smooth, about 10 minutes. Let stand, covered, for 30 minutes. Divide the dough into 12 equal pieces. Roll each piece into a ball, then into a 7.5cm (3in) round. Brush the top of 1 round lightly with:

Sesame or vegetable oil

Top with a second round. Roll out both rounds together into a 15cm (6in) pancake, being careful not to wrinkle the dough when rolling. Cook the pancakes in a lightly greased small frying pan over medium to medium-high heat until the surface blisters and turns the colour of parchment; turn often with chopsticks or tongs. Remove from the frying pan and immediately separate the pancakes, using a sharp knife. Repeat with the remaining disks. Keep the pancakes warm, loosely covered, in a very low oven.

At this point, the pancakes can be wrapped well and stored in the refrigerator or freezer. To reheat, arrange the pancakes slightly overlapping on a baking tray and bake, covered, at 150°C (300°F) Gas 2 until warm, 10 to 15 minutes. Combine and let stand until the mushrooms are softened, 15 to 20 minutes:

375ml (12floz) hot water

30g (1oz) dried shiitake mushrooms

7g (¼ oz) dried wood or cloud ear mushrooms

Drain, reserving the liquid, and squeeze out the excess water from the mushrooms. Slice the mushrooms, discarding the tough centres and stems. Combine:

250g (8oz) packet tempeh, cut into thin strips

1 tbsp light or dark soy sauce

Heat in a wok or large frying pan over medium heat:

1 tsp toasted sesame oil

Add:

3 large eggs, lightly beaten

Cook, without stirring, until set but still moist. Remove the egg pancake and cut into small pieces. Heat in the wok:

1 tbsp toasted sesame oil

Add the tempeh mixture and stir-fry until lightly browned. Add the mushrooms along with:

250g (8oz) tinned bamboo shoots, drained and sliced

4 tbsp sliced spring onions

2 tsp chopped peeled fresh ginger

Stir-fry for 2 to 3 minutes. Strain the mushroom soaking liquid through a fine-mesh sieve lined with dampened paper towels, measure it, and add water as needed to make 180ml (6floz). Combine with:

3 tbsp light or dark soy sauce

3 tbsp dry sherry

1 tbsp cornflour

1 tsp sugar

Pour into the wok and boil, stirring, until thickened, about 1 minute. Gently stir in the egg pieces. Spread each pancake with:

2-3 tsp plum sauce

Top each with about 5 tbsp of the tempeh mixture and then with:

1 spring onion

Roll up, folding in the bottom end for eating.

Szechuan-Style "Hacked" Tempeh

4 servings

Tempeh is made by inoculating cooked skinless split soybeans with Rhizopus oligosporus *bacteria, shaping the beans into cakes, and allowing them to ferment for about 24 hours. The resulting supple slabs are sealed and refrigerated, ready for sale. Tempeh replaces the chicken in this traditional dish. Served chilled, the ingredients are tossed with a peanut sauce.*

Combine and let stand for 15 to 30 minutes:

250g (8oz) tempeh, cut into 1cm (½ in) cubes
2 tbsp light or dark soy sauce
2-3 tsp chopped peeled fresh ginger
1 tsp finely chopped garlic
½ tsp Szechuan peppercorns, cracked

Heat in a wok or medium frying pan over medium heat:

1 tbsp vegetable oil

Add the tempeh mixture and cook, stirring, until browned. Let cool, then refrigerate until chilled.

Combine and arrange on a serving platter:

375g (12oz) sliced, seeded, peeled cucumbers
125g (4oz) chopped red peppers
4 tbsp sliced spring onions

Spoon the tempeh mixture over the vegetables. Stir together until smooth and drizzle over the tempeh mixture:

4 tbsp smooth peanut butter
2 tbsp light or dark soy sauce
2 tbsp rice vinegar
1 tbsp dry sherry
3-4 tsp toasted sesame oil
1 tsp chilli paste

Garnish with:

125g (4oz) chopped red peppers
4 tbsp sliced spring onions
4 tbsp chopped salted peanuts

Toss just before serving. If desired, serve with:

Chilled cooked rice noodles

ABOUT
PASTAS
& GRAINS

*T*hey say love comes when you least expect it, and that's what's been happening with grains. People pampered their whole lives with thick steaks, flashy salads, and rich desserts are suddenly finding that what they really crave are homely little wheat berries and bowls of creamy risotto.

Nowhere is our tendency to mix and match world flavours more evident than in our passion for pasta and noodles, which make up one of the largest and richest chapters in home cooking. Certainly Italy has made the greatest contribution. Italy's influence on our love affair with pasta is so great that the Italian word pasta has become a part of our everyday language. In this chapter, we use pasta to refer to pasta of Italian origin and noodles when referring to eastern European and Oriental dishes.

Fresh Sweetcorn Risotto with Basil, Tomato and Lime, 106

Pasta, Grains and Nutrition

Pasta is made from wheat. From a nutritional standpoint, it joins other grain foods as the foundation of healthy diets and is the basis of many traditional cuisines. Many people believe that pasta is fattening and try to avoid eating it. This is a misunderstanding, as pasta is composed mainly of starch and protein, both relatively low in calories compared to fat. Most pasta dishes contain sauce, cheese or vegetables that balance the starch and prevent unusual fluctuation in blood sugar levels. People who are concerned about calories should keep the portion sizes within reasonable limits, use tomato rather than cream sauces and add just small amounts of cheese.

Dried pasta and fresh pasta are not better or worse, only different. That venerable favourite, spaghetti, is always a dried pasta made of the strongest durum wheat and water, never egg. On the other hand, fettuccine are flour and egg noodles that are best when fresh. However, in every case, a packet of good-quality dried pasta is far better than any mediocre fresh pasta.

The quest for low-fat, high-fibre fare led to a much closer look at grains, which provide complex carbohydrates, protein, a very small amount of fat, many of the B-complex vitamins and an essential array of minerals. By eating the six to eleven daily servings of grains recommended in general dietary guidelines, you can consume the recommended amount of protein found in one to three small portions of meat, without the saturated fat and with much more fibre. The nutrition is more reliable if the grains are whole, varied and supplemented by beans and some dairy products.

All true grains are fruits of grasses, and thus whole kernels are sometimes called berries. They are composed of three basic parts: the nutrient-dense germ, or seed, which contains protein and some oil; the endosperm, comprising carbohydrates and protein; and the bran or high-fibre outer layer. Rice, barley and oats also have an inedible outer husk; wheat, rye, and corn do not. If you eat all parts of the grain, other than the husk, you get all the vitamins, minerals and other nutrients it contains – all the nourishment the seed needs to become a plant. It is common practice, however, to remove the bran and the germ and consume only the endosperm. White rice, for example, is endosperm only. So is the part of the wheat that is ground into white flour. Both these products are enriched with B vitamins and iron to replace, and even increase, the amounts lost when the bran and germ are discarded, but some things, including the vitamin E and fibre of the original, are left out.

Grains are much more alike than not, both in the cooking and the nutrition. Good health food shops and some supermarkets will stock more than a dozen distinct grains, including buckwheat and quinoa, which are not true grains, botanically speaking, but are similar enough to be treated as such.

Cooking Pasta

Fresh or dried, pasta should always be cooked in a large quantity of fiercely boiling salted water. Use about 1 tbsp salt per 3 litres (5 pints) water. Estimate 6 litres (10 pints) water per 500g (1lb) pasta, except for delicate filled pastas and very large pasta such as lasagne, which will need 9-12 litres (15-20 pints) water. In either case, cooking more than 1kg (2lb) of pasta at once invites problems of uneven cooking and draining. Adequate water and frequent stirring are the two keys to eliminating the problem of pasta sticking together. Adding oil to the water has little effect except to keep the pot from boiling over. Unless the strands are outrageously long and cannot fit into the pot without cracking, do not break pasta before cooking.

Since pasta cooks quickly and is at its best as soon as it is cooked, have everything ready before you start – the sauce prepared, a large colander set in the sink for draining, and a serving bowl and dishes warming in the oven. Once the salted water is rapidly boiling, add the pasta all at once. As soon as the pasta softens slightly, give it a stir, partially cover the pot, and let it continue to boil vigorously, stirring often to keep it from sticking together.

Different pastas have different cooking times, and the only test for doneness is to lift a piece from the pot and taste it. Italians consider the ideal state *al dente* (to the tooth), which means tender but firm – no raw flour taste and enough firmness to give a pleasing resistance to the bite. Start testing fresh pasta and very thin shapes after about 30 seconds, spaghetti and linguine after 4 minutes and thick macaroni after 8 minutes. Once the pasta tastes done, do not waste a moment – empty the pot immediately into the colander and quickly toss the colander to rid the pasta of as much water as possible.

Combine the drained pasta with its sauce over heat if possible, or simply toss the hot pasta and sauce in a warmed serving bowl. Either way, eat pasta hot without delay. Rinse pasta only if destined to be baked or to be eaten cool in a salad.

Cooking Grains

Grains can be simmered on the stovetop, in the oven or in the microwave (which won't save time but will yield predictably good texture, with no pot to wash). The pressure cooker can be a big time-saver with long-cooking wheat berries and hulled barley, but it is important to consult your owner's manual for instructions; some recommend against cooking any grains, and others require that the grain be cooked in a foil-covered bowl to prevent the possibility that loose bits of hull or starch will clog the steam vent.

Wheat berries and other large whole grains are commonly pre-soaked for 8 hours or overnight to hasten their cooking time. A soaking shortcut is to heat the grain and liquid to a full boil on top of the stove and simmer for 2 minutes; remove from the heat and let stand, covered, for 1 hour, until some kernels begin to split. Or microwave the grain and liquid in a covered casserole on high for 10 minutes and then on medium for 5 minutes; let stand, covered, for 1 hour. Either way, cooking the grain in the soaking water retains nutrients. Note that presoaking is not always called for when the grain is to be used in a salad, because a firmer texture is desired.

Be generous with the size and the width of the pot when cooking grains, as they will cook fluffier if not clumped together. With more than 250g (8oz) of grains, you will get fluffier results if you use a wide saucepan, a flameproof casserole, or even a deep frying pan with a tight lid. Fine-textured and small grains, such as cornmeal and amaranth, tend to stick to the pot and scorch if not stirred often, especially if cooked without fat. Using a double boiler or the microwave reduces the risk, as well as the need to stir as much, by removing the grain from direct heat. Oven baking yields consistently dry, fluffy results with rice and barley if the casserole is wide and heavy enough, because the heat comes from all sides and not just the bottom of the pot.

Buying and Storing Grains

An important general consideration is freshness. Any whole grain, for example, whether brown rice or millet, is much more perishable than a refined product such as white rice or pearl barley. While pearl barley will keep for at least 6 months in an airtight container in a cool pantry, millet should be refrigerated to be sure of preventing rancidity. So it is wise to buy these in a shop that does a heavy volume of business in whole grains and perhaps even keeps them in a specially cooled section. Products high in oil content, especially quinoa and wheat germ, turn rancid fast and should be refrigerated once you get them home or break the vacuum seal of the jar. Buy other whole grains in amounts you can use within 1 month and store them in tightly covered jars in the pantry or refrigerate or freeze them in freezer bags or sealed containers for up to 2 months. Signs of rancidity are an off odour before cooking and a bitter taste when cooked. Grains purchased loose usually need to be rinsed and picked over for bits of chaff or debris. Place the grain in a large fine-mesh sieve set in a pot large enough to hold it; rinse under cold water, raking the grain with your fingers. Let debris rise to the surface and remove it. Drain well. Grains sold in boxes are generally clean and ready for the pot.

Cooked grains can be refrigerated for at least 3 days – and a few days longer if cooked with water and not stock or other perishable ingredients. They reheat beautifully in the microwave. Spread portions on individual plates, cover with cling film, and microwave on high for 1 to 2 minutes per serving. To reheat a bowlful, sprinkle the surface lightly with water, cover with cling film or a lid and microwave on high for about 1½ minutes per 185g (6oz); stir before serving. To reheat on the stovetop, put a thin layer of water in a saucepan, add the grain and simmer, covered, over medium heat until hot.

TOASTING GRAINS

Toasting a grain before you simmer it in liquid brings out the fragrance. You can spread it in a heavy saucepan or frying pan and heat over medium heat, stirring often, until the grain smells rich and toasted, usually just a few minutes; be careful not to scorch the smallest grains, such as amaranth and millet. Heating or melting some oil or butter in the pan before you stir in and toast the grain will add flavour and help keep the kernels separate, for fluffier texture, when they cook; this preparation is called a pilaf and often includes vegetables lightly browned with the grain.

To toast grains in the oven, spread on a baking tray and bake in a pre-heated 180°C (350°F) Gas 4 oven for about 10 minutes, stirring once.

Spaghetti with Aubergine

4 to 8 servings

The sauce for this Sicilian dish can be made several hours ahead if desired.
The night or morning before cooking, spread on a baking tray lined with a double layer of paper towels:

1 medium aubergine, unpeeled, cut into 1cm (½in) cubes

Sprinkle generously with:

Salt

Cover with another double layer of paper towels. Set a chopping board or another baking tray on top and weigh down with heavy tin cans. Let the aubergine drain for at least 8 hours. Heat in a large frying pan over medium heat:

3 tbsp extra-virgin olive oil

Add the aubergine and cook, stirring, until tender and golden. Add and cook for about 15 seconds:

2 large cloves garlic, finely chopped

Add:

7 medium, ripe tomatoes, peeled, seeded and chopped

2 medium peppers, preferably yellow, roasted, peeled and seeded, 58, and finely chopped

Cook, stirring frequently, until the sauce is thickened, about 10 minutes. Stir in:

15g (½ oz) fresh basil leaves, coarsely chopped

1 tbsp drained capers

2 large green olives, preferably Sicilian, stoned and chopped

Salt and ground black pepper to taste

Meanwhile, bring to a rolling boil in a large pot:

6 litres (10 pints) water

2 tbsp salt

Add and cook until tender but firm:

500g (1lb) spaghetti

Drain the pasta and toss with the sauce. Cheese is not traditionally served with this dish.

Tagliatelle with Wilted Greens

4 to 8 servings

Make this dish as spicy as you like by using more or fewer chilli peppers. Remember, much of a chilli's heat is in the seeds, so that removing them will temper the dish.

Bring to a rolling boil in a large pot:

6 litres (10 pints) water

2 tbsp salt

Add and cook until tender but firm:

625g (1¼ lb) fresh tagliatelle, or 500g (1lb) dried

Meanwhile, heat in a large frying pan or wok over medium heat:

2-4 tbsp olive oil

Add and cook until barely coloured:

4 tbsp chopped onion

4 cloves garlic, chopped

1-3 fresh hot chilli peppers, seeded and finely diced

Increase the heat to high and drop in:

3 big handfuls fresh rocket or mixed tart salad greens

Cook, stirring, until the greens are wilted. Drain the pasta and toss it with the greens, adding:

Salt and ground black pepper to taste

Shavings of pecorino cheese or crumbled fresh goat's cheese

Serve immediately.

Egg Noodles with Brown Butter and Nuts

Place in a small pan:

125g (4oz) unsalted butter

Gradually brown the butter over medium heat until golden brown and a nutty aroma arises. Add, if desired, any one or all of the following:

4 tbsp chopped nuts, such as cashews, roasted peanuts, pecans, toasted almonds, pine nuts or toasted walnuts

1 tsp finely chopped garlic (optional)

1 tbsp chopped fresh herbs, or

1 tsp dried, such as thyme, basil, chives, parsley, oregano and/or tarragon (optional)

Grated zest of small lemon (optional)

Toss with:

500g (1lb) dried egg noodles, cooked until tender but firm

Use your imagination and see what is in your refrigerator and spice drawer.

Golden Courgettes and Pasta

4 to 6 servings

Steam until tender:

500g (1lb) summer squash, cut into 1cm (½in) batons or dice

Toss in a bowl with:

500g (1lb) mostaccioli, penne or macaroni, cooked and drained

125-180ml (4-6floz) *Pesto Sauce, above right*

Pesto Sauce

Enough for 500g (1lb) pasta

This classic sauce from Genoa needs to be made with fresh basil. Pesto is traditionally tossed with trenette, a flat ribbon pasta similar to linguine but fresh. If freezing, add the nuts and cheese after thawing.

Process to a rough paste in a food processor:

60g (2oz) fresh basil leaves

45g (1½ oz) pine nuts

2 medium cloves garlic, peeled

45g (1½ oz) grated Parmesan cheese

With the machine running, slowly pour through the feed tube:

125ml (4floz) extra-virgin olive oil

If the sauce seems dry (it should be a thick paste), add a little more olive oil. Season with:

Salt and ground black pepper to taste

Use immediately or store in a covered glass jar in the refrigerator for up to 1 week.

Aubergine Lasagne Bundles

4 to 8 servings

Peel, if desired, and cut into 1cm (½in) rounds:

1kg (2lb) aubergine

Steam the aubergine in batches over boiling salted water until very soft but still intact, 10 to 15 minutes. Spread the cooked slices on a platter and sprinkle with:

½ tsp sea salt

For the béchamel, melt in a saucepan over medium-low heat:

90g (3oz) unsalted butter

With a wooden spoon, stir in:

6 tbsp plain flour

Cook, stirring, until the mixture has bubbled and cooked for 2 minutes to remove the raw taste of the flour. Do not allow the flour to darken. Off the heat, gradually whisk in:

750ml (24floz) milk

When the milk is completely incorporated, continue to whisk until smooth and lump free. Cook, stirring, over low heat until the béchamel has thickened to the consistency of thick cream. If you notice any lumps in the sauce, strain the béchamel through a fine-mesh sieve and transfer to a clean pan. Add:

4 tbsp tomato purée

½ tsp sea salt

Whisk until smooth. Set aside, whisking every 5 minutes to prevent a skin from forming. Preheat the oven to 190°C (375°F) Gas 5. Smear a 30 x 23cm (12 x 9in) dish with:

30g (1oz) unsalted butter

Bring to a boil in a large pot:

6 litres (10 pints) water

Generously salt the water and add in 2 or 3 batches:

8 sheets fresh lasagne or equivalent of good-quality imported dried lasagne

The fresh pasta will cook in 30 seconds after the water has resumed boiling. Scoop the pasta sheets from the pot with a strainer and let drain in a colander. Lay them out on a clean work surface. Spread each sheet with 1 to 2 tbsp of the béchamel. On the bottom half of each sheet, lay out the cooked aubergine slices, then cover them with:

375g (12oz) fresh mozzarella, thinly sliced

60g (2oz) grated Parmesan cheese

Fold the top half of the pasta over the aubergine and cheese, spread the surface of each bundle with an additional 1 tbsp béchamel, if desired, then fold each side in towards the middle. You now have a rectangular pasta bundle. Spread half of the remaining béchamel sauce over the bottom of the buttered pan. Top with the pasta bundles, seam-side down, overlapping them a bit if necessary. Top with the remaining béchamel and sprinkle over the surface:

30g (1oz) grated Parmesan cheese

Dot with:

30g (1oz) unsalted butter, cut into bits

Bake for 15 minutes. Increase the oven temperature to 200°C (400°F) Gas 6 and bake until a golden crust forms on top, about 5 minutes more. Remove from the oven and let rest for 5 to 10 minutes before serving.

Roast Vegetable Lasagne

8 to 10 servings

The vegetables in this lasagne are first roasted, giving them extra flavour and character. They can be prepared a day ahead and stored in the refrigerator. This version is made without the traditional tomato sauce, incorporating fresh tomatoes into the layers instead. The courgettes and aubergine are roasted together, divided between two tins, while the tomatoes are roasted in their own pan because they release a lot of juice, which would inhibit browning of the courgettes and aubergine. If your oven will hold two tins side by side, then you will be able to roast everything at the same time on two racks. If not, roast the tomatoes as a separate batch. The lasagne is covered during a portion of the baking time because there is no tomato sauce; use a layer of breadcrumbs if desired.

Position a rack in the lower third of the oven and another in the upper third. Preheat the oven to 230°C (450°F) Gas 8. Lightly oil a 33 x 23 x 7.5cm (13 x 9 x 3in) baking or lasagne dish.

Place in a large bowl:

2 medium-large aubergines (about 1.5kg/3lb), quartered and cut into 1cm (½in) slices

6 medium courgettes (about 1.5kg/3lb), cut into 1cm (½in) slices

Pour over the vegetables:

125ml (4floz) olive oil, preferably extra-virgin

1 tsp salt

½ tsp ground black pepper

Toss well to coat all the vegetable pieces with oil and remove to 2 roasting tins. Position the tins side by side in the oven or place 1 on each rack if they do not fit side by side. Roast for 20 minutes. Toss the vegetables with a metal spatula, scraping up the browned bits. Continue to roast until well browned and soft, about 20 minutes more. Remove to a large bowl. Place in a roasting tin:

1.5kg (3lb) ripe tomatoes, halved crosswise

Drizzle over the tomatoes:

2 tbsp extra-virgin olive oil

Generous amount of salt

Ground black pepper to taste

Roast the tomatoes until soft and slightly golden, about 45 minutes. Remove the tomatoes with their juice and all the oil to the bowl with the vegetables and stir together well. Reduce the oven temperature to 190°C (375°F) Gas 5.

Bring to a rolling boil in a large pot:

8 litres (13 pints) water

2 tbsp salt

Meanwhile, stir together well in a medium bowl:

500g (1lb) ricotta cheese

2 large eggs

45g (1½ oz) grated Parmesan

½ tsp salt, or to taste

Ground black pepper to taste

Ground nutmeg to taste (optional)

Have ready:

500g (1lb) mozzarella cheese (preferably fresh), grated

When the water boils, add and cook until barely tender:

500g (1lb) fresh, or 500g (1lb) dried lasagne

Drain and separate the pasta sheets. Keep in a bowl of iced water. To assemble the lasagne, arrange a layer of pasta over the bottom of the prepared pan. Spread with one-third of the ricotta mixture. Sprinkle one-quarter of the mozzarella over the ricotta mixture along with:

2 tbsp Parmesan cheese

Ground black pepper to taste

Spoon one-third of the roast vegetables on top. Add another layer of pasta and continue layering the lasagne until all the ingredients are used. You will have 4 layers of pasta and 3 layers of filling. Sprinkle the final one-quarter of the mozzarella over the top along with:

2 tbsp Parmesan cheese

90g (3oz) fresh breadcrumbs (optional)

Cover the pan with foil and bake for 30 minutes. Uncover and continue to bake until golden and bubbly, about 15 minutes more. Let stand for 15 minutes before serving.

AUBERGINES

The peak season for aubergines is midsummer to midautumn. Select aubergines of whatever sort that are heavy for their size, with taut skin, a fresh, green cap and stem and not a single soft spot, cut or bruise. In standard types, the skin should be glossy. As a rule, small to medium aubergines are the choicest, being the youngest. If the aubergine seems old and the flesh is dark, it may need salting to draw out its bitterness. Generously sprinkle pieces with coarse salt. Place them in a nonreactive colander and let drain for 30 to 60 minutes. Turn onto a thick tea towel and gently press out excess moisture. Lightly rub the pieces in the tea towel to rub off the salt and dry them.

ELECTRIC RICE COOKERS

Electric rice cookers are ingenious devices that make preparing white or brown rice a snap. Most rice cookers have a large cooking chamber (often lined with a non-stick coating) that rests above an electric heating element. Most also come with a perforated insert that fits near the bottom of the cooking pot, transforming the rice cooker into a steamer for vegetables, fish and other foods. Follow the manufacturer's instructions, but keep in mind that some rice cookers imported from Asia come with directions that assume the rice has been rinsed or soaked. When cooking dry – not rinsed or soaked – rice in a rice cooker, use 60-125ml (2-4floz) less water per 220g (7oz) than you would in stovetop cooking.

Basic Cooked White Rice

4 servings

A cook needs to know two things about rice. The first is whether or not the bran and germ are still attached. If so, it is brown rice, making it more nutritious, more perishable and slower cooking than white rice. The second thing is the length of the grain. The longer the grain, the less starchy and plump the rice. Use 500ml (16floz) water for soft, tender rice or 430-460ml (14-15floz) for firmer grains. Use 60ml (2floz) less, either way, when cooking medium-grain white rice. Do not stir, except as directed, as the rice will turn gummy.

I. Bring to a boil in a medium saucepan:

430-500ml (14-16floz) water
15g (½ oz) butter or 1 tbsp
    vegetable oil (optional)
¼ to ½ tsp salt

Add and stir once:

220g (7oz) long-grain white rice

Cover and cook over very low heat until all the water is absorbed, 15 to 18 minutes. Do not lift the cover before the end of cooking. Let stand, covered, for 5 to 10 minutes before serving.

II. This method is popular in the American South, Latin America and parts of Europe. Spread in a large, broad, shallow, heavy saucepan to a depth of only 2 or 3 grains:

220g (7oz) long-grain or
    medium-grain white rice

Add just enough liquid to cover the rice by 1cm (½ in) or the thickness of your hand. Bring to a gentle boil and stir once. Cook, uncovered, over low heat until the liquid is almost absorbed, about 5 minutes. Cover the saucepan and continue to cook for 15 to 18 minutes. Do not lift the cover before the end of cooking. Let stand, covered, for 5 to 10 minutes before serving.

Fried Rice

4 servings

Fried rice is popular as much for its taste as for its rapid preparation and versatility. Remember to always begin with cold cooked rice (a mixture of part white and part brown is excellent). The variations are endless. Add small amounts (about 60g/2oz) of cooked cut-up broccoli, carrots, green beans, courgettes or sweet potatoes or thawed frozen green peas. For additional flavour, sprinkle with toasted sesame seeds or chopped peanuts. Drizzle with toasted sesame oil or soy sauce at the table.

Whisk together:

4 eggs

½ tsp salt

Heat a large frying pan or wok over medium heat until hot enough to evaporate a drop of water on contact. Pour in and tilt the pan to coat:

1 tbsp vegetable oil

Heat until very hot. Add the eggs all at once and as they bubble up around the edges, push them to the centre, tilting the frying pan to cook the eggs evenly. Break the cooked eggs into clumps. When the eggs are set, remove to a bowl. Pour into the hot frying pan and heat until hot:

2 tbsp vegetable oil

Add and cook, stirring to coat the grains with oil, for 3 minutes:

375-500g (12oz-1lb) cold cooked rice (220-280g/7-9oz uncooked)

1 tsp chopped peeled fresh ginger

Stir in the cooked eggs along with:

60g (2oz) thin spring onion slices

Serve immediately.

Thai Coconut Rice

4 to 6 servings

Thai, or jasmine, rice is a long-grain rice with a soft, slightly sticky consistency. If using American grown jasmine rice, there is no need to rinse it. Asian jasmine rice should probably be rinsed. Tinned unsweetened coconut milk is available in many supermarkets or wherever Asian groceries are sold.

Bring to a boil in a large saucepan:

250ml (8floz) tinned unsweetened coconut milk and 250ml (8floz) water

220g (7oz) jasmine rice

1 thin slice peeled fresh ginger

¾ tsp salt

Stir once, cover and cook over very low heat until the liquid is absorbed and the rice is tender, about 20 minutes.

Meanwhile lightly toast, stirring, in a small frying pan over medium-low heat:

15g (½ oz) grated unsweetened dried coconut

Sprinkle over the cooked rice along with:

Fresh coriander leaves (optional)

Persian Rice

4 to 6 servings

Prepare in a nonstick frying pan so the rice can be easily inverted, showing off its deliciously crisp crust.

Preheat the oven to 180°C (350°F) Gas 4.

Bring to a boil in a large pot:

4 litres (6½ pints) water
1 tbsp salt

Stir in:

440g (14oz) white basmati rice
2.5cm (1in) cinnamon stick
3 whole cloves
3 black peppercorns
¼ tsp cardamom pods

Cook, uncovered, stirring occasionally, until the rice is almost tender, about 10 minutes. Drain and let stand in a sieve until ready to use. (Leave the spices in the rice.) Melt in a large ovenproof nonstick frying pan over medium heat:

125g (4oz) butter

Spoon off 3 tbsp and reserve. Add to the remaining butter in the pan:

90g (3oz) thinly sliced onions
¼ tsp saffron threads

Cook, stirring, over medium heat until the onions are golden, about 8 minutes. Spread the onions in an even layer in the frying pan. Stir into the cooked rice:

2 tbsp diced dried apricots
2 tbsp dried sweet or sour cherries or sultanas

Spoon the rice over the onions; smooth the top of the rice with the back of a large spoon and press down very firmly to pack it. Drizzle the reserved butter evenly over the top. Cover with a double layer of foil, crimping the edges and pressing down on the top. Bake for 1 hour. Let stand, covered, for 10 minutes. Uncover and invert a large round platter over the frying pan. Protecting your hands with a tea towel, turn the frying pan and platter over, allowing the rice to drop onto the platter.

Sprinkle with:

4 tbsp chopped shelled pistachios

Basic Pilaf

4 servings

Rice stirred in hot butter or oil before simmering is very flavourful and fluffy, especially if you use basmati rice. The preparation is known as a pilaf, and it traditionally calls for seasonings to be sautéed in the pot with the rice. The name can be traced to the Persian pilau. All kinds of variations are found in the Middle East, the Caucasus and India.

Melt in a large saucepan or deep frying pan over low heat:

30g (1oz) butter

Add and cook, stirring, until golden, about 8 minutes:

60g (2oz) chopped onions

Add and cook, stirring, until coated, about 3 minutes:

220g (7oz) white basmati rice

Stir in:

500ml (16floz) water or *Vegetable Stock*, 17

½ tsp salt (if using water)

Bring to a boil. Stir once, cover and cook over low heat until the liquid is absorbed and the rice is tender, about 15 minutes. Do not stir. Let stand, covered, for 5 minutes before serving. Sprinkle with:

2 tbsp chopped walnuts, toasted, or 2 tbsp chopped fresh parsley

Two-Grain Date Pilaf

4 to 6 servings

Rice and bulgur spiced with a cinnamon stick and topped with a few chopped dates make this recipe an especially exotic pilaf.

Melt in a large saucepan or deep frying pan over medium heat:

30g (1oz) butter

Add and cook, stirring, until golden, about 8 minutes:

60g (2oz) chopped onions

Add:

220g (7oz) white basmati rice

100g (3½ oz) bulgur or cracked wheat

2.5cm (1in) cinnamon stick

Stir to coat with the butter. Add:

1 litre (1½ pints) water or *Vegetable Stock*, 17

1 tsp salt (if using water)

Bring to a boil. Stir once, cover and cook over medium-low heat until the liquid is absorbed and the rice is tender, about 20 minutes. Uncover and let stand for 5 minutes. Meanwhile, melt in a small frying pan over medium heat:

15g (½ oz) butter

Add and cook, stirring, until heated through, about 1 minute:

4 tbsp diced dates

Spoon the pilaf into a serving dish and top with the dates. Serve immediately.

Lentil and Rice Pilaf with Toasted Cumin Seeds

4 to 6 servings

Whole cumin seeds lend a wonderful aroma to this dish. Serve as a side dish or as a main course topped with cooked vegetables.

Stir into a medium saucepan of boiling water:

90g (3oz) lentils, picked over and rinsed

Boil, uncovered, for 10 minutes; drain. Heat in a large saucepan or deep frying pan over low heat:

2 tbsp vegetable oil

Add and cook just until sizzling, about 1 minute:

1 clove garlic, finely chopped

½ tsp cumin seeds

Add the lentils along with:

220g (7oz) white basmati rice

Stir to combine. Add:

500ml (16floz) *Vegetable Stock*, 17

¼ to ½ tsp salt

Bring to a boil. Stir once, cover and cook over medium-low heat until the stock is absorbed and the rice and lentils are tender, about 15 minutes. Uncover and let stand for 5 minutes. Meanwhile, toast in a small frying pan over medium heat:

4 tbsp chopped walnuts

Sprinkle over the pilaf and serve.

Wild Rice with Sautéed Mushrooms

4 to 6 servings

Use any combination of exotic and/or cultivated mushrooms in this simple dish.

Combine in a large saucepan:

750ml (24floz) water

185g (6oz) wild rice, rinsed and drained

1 tsp salt (optional)

Bring to a boil. Stir once, cover and simmer over low heat until the water is absorbed and the rice is fluffy and tender, 35 to 55 minutes. About 10 minutes before the rice is done, heat in a large saucepan or frying pan over medium-high heat:

60ml (2floz) olive oil

Add and cook, stirring, until lightly browned, 5 to 8 minutes:

250g (8oz) sliced button or chestnut mushrooms

125g (4oz) sliced shiitake or porcini mushroom caps

125g (4oz) chopped onions

Add and cook, stirring, until combined, about 2 minutes:

4 tbsp finely chopped fresh parsley

2 cloves garlic, finely chopped

1 tsp fresh thyme, or ¼ tsp dried

Stir in the cooked wild rice along with:

Salt and ground black pepper to taste

Cover and cook over medium heat until heated through, about 5 minutes. If desired, sprinkle with:

4 tbsp sliced unblanched almonds, toasted

Oven-Baked Brown Rice with Mushrooms

4 to 6 servings

Brown rice and mushrooms share the same deep, earthy flavour. Serve this simple preparation topped with broccoli or a mixture of cooked vegetables.
Preheat the oven to 180°C (350°F) Gas 4. Melt or heat in a 2 litre (3 pint) stovetop-to-oven casserole over medium-high heat:

45g (1½ oz) butter or 3 tbsp olive oil

Add and cook, stirring, until the mushrooms are lightly browned, about 8 minutes:

250g (8oz) coarsely chopped mushrooms
60g (2oz) chopped onions
1 clove garlic, finely chopped
Add and stir until coated:
250g (8oz) long-grain brown rice
⅛ tsp ground black pepper
Add:
560ml (18floz) *Vegetable Stock, 17*
¼ tsp salt
Bring to a boil. Cover and bake until the rice is tender and the stock is absorbed, about 45 minutes. Let stand, covered, for 10 minutes before serving.

Barley and Mushroom "Risotto"

8 servings

This is not a real risotto because it does not contain rice, but it is made in the same way. To serve this dish as a main course for 4 people, omit the salt and stir in 45 to 90g (1½ to 3oz) grated Parmesan cheese just before serving.
Heat in a large, deep frying pan over medium heat until the foam subsides:

60-90g (2-3oz) butter
Add and cook, stirring, until tender but not brown, about 7 minutes:
155g (5oz) finely chopped onions
Stir in and cook until softened:
250g (8oz) shiitake mushrooms, stems removed and caps diced
Reduce the heat to medium-low. Add and stir until glazed with butter:
220g (7oz) pearl barley
Add and cook, stirring, until the liquid is absorbed:

160ml (5floz) dry white wine
1 tbsp crushed or finely chopped garlic
½ tsp salt
½ tsp ground black pepper
Warm, but do not allow to simmer, in a saucepan set over very low heat:
1.5 litres (2½ pints) *Vegetable Stock, 17*
Keep the stock warm. Stir 500ml (16floz) of the vegetable stock into the barley. Simmer slowly, stirring occasionally, until the stock is almost absorbed. Add the remaining stock 125ml (4floz) at a time, allowing each addition to be absorbed before adding the next and stirring often. The barley needs 45 to 60 minutes' cooking to become tender. If you run low on stock while the barley is still very underdone, reduce the heat. If you do run out of stock, finish cooking with hot water.

Fresh Sweetcorn Risotto with Basil, Tomato and Lime

4 to 6 servings

The lime juice adds a distinctive flavour when combined with the natural acidity of the tomato and the sweet, starchy taste of the sweetcorn and the rice.
Combine:

185g (6oz) diced, seeded, peeled ripe tomatoes
2 tbsp chopped fresh basil
1 tbsp fresh lime juice
¼ tsp salt, or to taste
Bring to a simmer:
1.25 litres (2 pints) *Vegetable Stock*, 17
Cut:
375g (12oz) sweetcorn kernels from 4 or 5 large ears
Purée half the sweetcorn kernels in a food processor. Heat in a large saucepan or deep frying pan over medium heat until the foam subsides:
30g (1oz) unsalted butter
Add and cook, stirring, until translucent, about 5 minutes:
90g (3oz) finely chopped spring onions (white part only)
Add:
345g (11oz) Italian or medium-grain rice

Stir to coat with the butter. Add:
125ml (4floz) dry white wine
Cook, stirring, until absorbed. Add 250ml (8floz) of the simmering stock and cook, stirring, over medium-low heat until the stock is absorbed. Add the remaining stock, 125ml (4floz) at a time, cooking and stirring until the liquid is almost completely absorbed before adding more, about 15 minutes in all. Stir in the reserved puréed sweetcorn and another 125ml (4floz) stock; continue to cook, stirring and adding stock as needed, until the rice is tender but with a slight firmness to the centre of the grain, 5 to 10 minutes more, or longer, depending on the rice. Stir in the sweetcorn kernels and the fresh tomato mixture. Season with:
Salt and ground black pepper to taste
Spoon into warmed soup bowls and sprinkle each serving with:
Grated Parmesan cheese

RULES FOR RISOTTO

- Use a large, heavy saucepan and never cover the cooking risotto. Anticipate about 20 minutes' cooking time.

- Use a medium-grain rice, never long-grain. First choices are Italian imports, always "superfino" grade – Arborio, Carnaroli, Vialone Nano, Roma, or Balso.

- Add small quantities of simmering stock to the risotto and stir almost constantly.

- At the end of cooking, the rice should be creamy in consistency and tender to the taste but still have a little "bite". Let the risotto stand off the heat for a few minutes before serving.

Leftover Risotto Pancake (Risotto al Salto)

4 servings

Place in a large bowl:
250-500ml (8-16floz) cold leftover risotto, *above and opposite*
Stir in, 1 tbsp at a time:
1 large egg, lightly beaten
If the risotto is very soft, do not add all of the egg. Heat in a large nonstick frying pan over medium-low heat until foamy:
30g (1oz) butter
Add the risotto mixture by tablespoonfuls for small pancakes or by large serving spoonful measures for larger pancakes. Cook, undisturbed, until the bottoms are browned and crisp, about 5 minutes. Carefully turn and brown the second side, about 5 minutes. If making small pancakes, several can be fried at once, but fry larger pancakes 1 at a time. Before serving, sprinkle with:
Grated Parmesan cheese

Risotto Primavera

8 first-course servings; 6 main-course servings

This makes a great first or main course.
Combine and let stand for
10 minutes:

**3 generous pinches of saffron
threads**

250ml (8floz) hot *Vegetable Stock,* **17**

Melt in a large, heavy saucepan over
medium heat:

45g (1½ oz) butter

Stir in:

1 medium onion, finely chopped

Cook over low heat until soft and
clear. Meanwhile, simmer over
medium heat:

2.25 litres (3½ pints) *Vegetable
Stock,* **17**

Increase the heat under the onions
to medium and stir in:

**500g (1lb) Italian or medium-
grain rice**

Cook, stirring often, until the rice
is chalky in appearance, about
5 minutes. Add:

125ml (4floz) dry white wine

Stir until absorbed. Add the saffron
mixture and simmer, uncovered,
stirring often, until absorbed. Add
the vegetable stock, 250ml (8floz)
at a time, and simmer and stir
continuously until absorbed. (If
desired, when half of the stock has
been used and the rice is still quite
firm, the risotto can be removed
from the heat and refrigerated,
covered, for up to 2 days. To finish
the risotto, reheat and continue.)
Add the remaining stock, 250ml
(8floz) at a time, until the rice is
tender but still has some "bite". It
should be creamy and not stiff.
Fold in:

90-155g (3-5oz) grated Parmesan

**250g (8oz) sautéed spring vegetables,
cut into bite-sized pieces**

Season with:

**Salt and ground black pepper
to taste**

Let rest for a few minutes,
then serve in warmed soup dishes.
If desired, serve with:

Grated Parmesan cheese

Oven-Baked Polenta

6 servings

In this version of polenta, the preliminary cooking can be cut in half because the polenta finishes cooking as it bakes in the oven.
Melt or heat in a large saucepan over medium heat:

30g (1oz) butter or 2 tbsp olive oil
Add and cook, stirring, until translucent, about 5 minutes:

75g (2½ oz) finely chopped onions
Stir in and bring to a boil:

750ml (24floz) water, or 375ml (12floz) *Vegetable Stock*, 17, and 375ml (12floz) water
Stir together:

500ml (16floz) water, or 250ml (8floz) *Vegetable Stock*, 17, and 250ml (8floz) water
185g (6oz) polenta
Gradually stir into the boiling liquid; cook, stirring constantly, over low heat until the polenta is thickened, about 15 minutes. Preheat the oven to 180°C (350°F) Gas 4. Lightly butter a shallow 2 litre (3 pint) baking dish. Pour half of the polenta into the baking dish. Smooth with a spatula. Have ready:

125g (4oz) Gruyère cheese, thinly slivered
125g (4oz) mozzarella cheese, thinly slivered
45g (1½ oz) grated Parmesan
Top the layer of polenta with half of the cheese. Spread the remaining polenta on top and sprinkle with the remaining cheese. Pour over:

125ml (4floz) double cream, single cream or milk
Bake until the top is browned and bubbly, 35 to 45 minutes. Let stand for 10 minutes before serving.

Posole

4 servings

Posole is a hearty Latin American stew served on feast days and other special occasions. This is one of many variations on a piquant classic. The day before cooking the posole, start the chilli paste.
Place in a bowl and cover with boiling water by 2.5cm (1in).

6-8 dried New Mexico (red Anaheim) peppers, seeded
6-8 dried chilli negro (also called chilaca) peppers, seeded
Soak for at least 8 hours or overnight. Drain and finely chop in a food processor, then press through a food mill or sieve. Refrigerate until ready to use.
For the posole, heat in a large saucepan over medium heat:

1 tbsp olive oil
Add and cook, stirring, until translucent, about 5 minutes:

125g (4oz) chopped onions
Add and cook, stirring, until the chillies are softened, about 3 minutes:

125g (4oz) chopped red peppers
1 tbsp chopped garlic
½ tsp dried oregano
Stir in:

375g (12oz) drained tinned hominy or thawed frozen hominy
500ml (16floz) *Vegetable Stock*, 17
Bring to a boil. Stir in 4 to 5 tbsp (to taste) of the chilli paste with:

4 tbsp chopped seeded fresh Anaheim peppers or tinned green chilli peppers
1 tbsp chopped seeded fresh jalapeño peppers
Simmer, partially covered, over low heat for 30 minutes. Just before serving, stir in:

80ml (3floz) fresh orange juice
2 tbsp fresh lemon juice
1 tsp salt, or to taste
Serve over rice.

HOMINY

Dried sweetcorn that has been treated with an alkali to remove its hulls is called hominy or slaked corn. The process makes the niacin in corn available as a nutrient and thus prevents pellagra. The Native Americans who first made hominy used wood ash or lime; today slaked lime or lye is most common. Cracked into a coarse meal, hominy becomes hominy grits; ground into flour, it is masa harina, used to make tortillas. Whole dried hominy made from white corn is also known as posole; cooked, it is available tinned and, in some places, frozen. Hominy is sometimes available as golden (made from yellow corn) and white. Dried hominy needs to be soaked overnight, drained and simmered until tender before use. Tinned needs only to be rinsed before use.

Quinoa-Stuffed Acorn Squash

4 servings

Quinoa, pronounced "keenwa", was cultivated in the Andes by Inca farmers. Botanically, it is not a true grain, but a relative of spinach and beetroot. Quinoa can be substituted for bulgur or white rice in pilafs and salads.

Preheat the oven to 180°C (350°F) Gas 4.

Place cut side down in a baking tin:

3 acorn squash, halved and seeded

Add 1cm (½ in) water to the tin and cover with foil. Bake until the squash are tender, 45 to 55 minutes. Leave the oven on. Let the squash cool. Heat in a large frying pan over medium heat:

15g (½ oz) butter

Add and cook, stirring, until golden, about 8 minutes:

60g (2oz) chopped onions

Stir in:

60g (2oz) quinoa, rinsed and drained

Heat, stirring, until toasted, about 3 minutes. Stir in:

250ml (8floz) *Vegetable Stock, 17*

Bring to a boil, reduce the heat, and simmer, covered, for 15 minutes. Uncover and let cool slightly. Scoop out and dice the pulp of 2 squash halves. Turn the other 4 halves cut side up and season with:

½ tsp salt

⅛ tsp ground black pepper

Combine the quinoa and diced squash. Stir in:

30g (1oz) chopped hazelnuts or whole unblanched almonds, toasted

2 tbsp chopped fresh parsley

2 tbsp grated Parmesan cheese

Spoon into the 4 squash cavities, distributing evenly. Sprinkle the tops with:

2 tbsp grated Parmesan cheese

Bake until heated through, about 20 minutes.

Whole-Grain Berries with Sautéed Onions and Dried Fruits

4 servings

Fully cooked whole-grain berries make an excellent dish when tossed with golden sautéed onions and plumped diced dried fruits.

Soak in water to cover by 5cm (2in):

185g (6oz) wheat, spelt or kamut berries or a combination

Let stand overnight. Drain if needed and add to:

2 litres (3¼ pints) boiling salted water

Gently simmer, uncovered, until tender but still chewy, 45 to 60 minutes. Drain. Melt or heat in a large frying pan over medium heat:

30g (1oz) butter or 2 tbsp olive oil

Add and cook, stirring, until golden, 8 to 10 minutes:

125g (4oz) chopped onions

Add:

185g (6oz) diced mixed dried fruits, such as dried apricots, stoned prunes, sultanas, currants, dried cherries and/or dried cranberries

Stir to blend. Stir in:

Cooked wheat, spelt or kamut berries

5cm (2in) cinnamon stick

125ml (4floz) *Vegetable Stock*, 17, or water

Cover and cook, stirring once or twice, over low heat until the flavours are blended, about 10 minutes. Season with:

¼ tsp salt

⅛ tsp ground black pepper

If desired, sprinkle with:

30g (1oz) chopped blanched almonds, walnuts or pecans, toasted

Bowties with Kasha (Kasha Varnishkes)

4 to 8 servings

Kasha Varnishkes is a traditional eastern European dish that is low in calories and delicious. The trick to making tender but firm, not mushy, kasha is to coat it with egg and stir it over high heat until toasted and the grains are separate. The nutty flavour of the kasha is a wonderful foil for the creamy taste of pasta. In the summer, we turn this dish into a pasta salad using whatever fresh vegetables can be found and toss with a vinaigrette dressing. Rigatoni or small shells work well here too.

Brown in a medium nonstick frying pan over medium-high heat:

2-3 tbsp vegetable oil

2 large onions, cut into 1cm (½in) pieces

250g (8oz) sliced mushrooms (button, shiitake or portobello, or a combination), optional

1 clove garlic, finely chopped

Salt and ground black pepper to taste

Remove to a large bowl. Cook in a large pot of boiling salted water until tender but firm:

185g (6oz) bowtie pasta

Drain the noodles and toss with the onion mixture. Beat in a small bowl:

1 large egg

Add:

220g (7oz) whole kasha (whole roast buckwheat groats)

Stir until the grains are well coated. Wipe out the pan and heat it over high heat. Transfer the kasha mixture to the pan and cook, stirring, until the grains are toasted and separate, 2 to 3 minutes. Reduce the heat to low and add:

500ml (16floz) hot *Vegetable Stock*, 17

Stir, cover, and simmer until the stock is absorbed and the kasha is tender but not mushy, 7 to 8 minutes. Stir in the noodle mixture. Taste and adjust the seasonings. Garnish with:

2 tbsp chopped fresh parsley

Serve immediately. The dish can be made 1 to 2 days in advance and reheated, uncovered, in a 180°C (350°F) Gas 4 oven. If the mixture is dry, add 60ml (2floz) more vegetable stock.

BUCKWHEAT

The nuttiness of the kernels makes Russia's roast buckwheat groats, or kasha, irresistible. Buy kasha, commonly sold in supermarkets, for deepest flavour, or choose unroasted groats, found in health food shops, for blander delicacy.

Baked Courgettes Stuffed with Couscous

4 servings

Preheat the oven to 200°C (400°F) Gas 6. Lightly oil a baking dish. Trim the stems and halve lengthwise:

2 medium courgettes

Sprinkle with:

**Salt and ground black pepper
    to taste**

Place the courgettes cut side down in the baking dish. Bake until the cut side is lightly browned, 10 to 12 minutes. Reduce the oven temperature to 180°C (350°F) Gas 4. Let the courgettes cool slightly. Using a teaspoon, scoop out the centres of the courgettes, leaving four 5mm (¼ in) shells. Finely chop the pulp. Heat in a large frying pan over medium heat:

1 tbsp extra-virgin olive oil

Add and cook, stirring, until golden, about 5 minutes:

4 tbsp chopped onions

Add the chopped courgettes along with:

**60g (2oz) quick-cooking,
    wholewheat, or spelt couscous**
1 clove garlic, finely chopped

Cook, stirring, until coated with the oil. Stir in:

180ml (6floz) *Vegetable Stock, 17*
1 tbsp currants
½ tsp ground cinnamon

Bring to a boil. Cover and cook over low heat for 5 minutes. Uncover and let cool to room temperature. Stir in:

1 tbsp pine nuts, toasted

Spoon the couscous mixture into the courgette boats, dividing it evenly. Arrange in the baking dish and cover with foil. Bake until heated through, about 20 minutes. Serve hot.

Couscous with Courgettes and Cherry Tomatoes

6 servings

A good dish for summer.

Heat in a large saucepan over medium-low heat:

2 tbsp olive oil

Add and cook, stirring, until golden, about 5 minutes:

1 medium onion, chopped

Add and cook, stirring, for 1 minute:

2 cloves garlic, finely chopped

Stir in:

625ml (1 pint) *Vegetable Stock, 17*
**750g (1½ lb) medium courgettes,
    trimmed and cut into 1cm
    (½ in) slices**

Bring to a boil. Cook until the courgettes are tender but not soft, 3 to 5 minutes. Stir in:

**2 tbsp chopped fresh thyme, or
    2 tsp dried**

Stir in:

**280g (9oz) quick-cooking
    couscous**
15g (½ oz) butter or 1 tbsp olive oil

Remove from the heat. Cover and let stand until the stock is absorbed, about 10 minutes. Fluff the couscous with a fork. Stir in:

24 cherry tomatoes

Serve.

Winter Vegetable Couscous

10 to 12 servings

This dish is delicious with Harissa *(below left), the Moroccan chilli-pepper condiment.* Ras El Hanout *(below right) is added to both the vegetables and to the couscous.* Heat in a medium frying pan until moderately hot but not smoking:

60ml (2floz) olive oil

Add and cook, stirring, until softened and just beginning to brown:

3 portobello mushrooms, wiped clean, gills removed and thickly sliced

Remove from the heat and set aside. Heat in a large, heavy pan until moderately hot but not smoking:

60ml (2floz) olive oil

Add:

1 red onion, quartered

1 celeriac, cut into large chunks

2 white turnips, peeled and quartered

1 swede, peeled and cut into 5cm (2in) pieces

2 leeks (white and green parts), cleaned thoroughly and cut into 5mm (¼ in) slices

1 medium head cauliflower, separated into florets

½ tsp dried thyme

½ tsp dried marjoram

Stir in:

1 tbsp *Ras El Hanout*, below

Cook, covered, over medium heat until partially cooked, about 10 minutes. Stir in:

750ml (24floz) *Vegetable Stock, 17*

Continue cooking until the vegetables are tender but not overdone, 20 to 30 minutes. At the end of the cooking, the flavours of the vegetables should have blended together well, but each one should hold together and be distinct. During the last 10 minutes of cooking, stir in the reserved portobello mushrooms along with:

375g (12oz) cooked chickpeas, rinsed and drained if tinned

Season with:

Salt and ground black pepper to taste

Rinse in a sieve with tap water:

1kg (2lb) couscous

Transfer to a large saucepan and stir in:

2 tbsp *Ras El Hanout*, below

Salt to taste

Let stand for 20 minutes, then rub the couscous through your hands to separate the grains. Ten minutes before serving, stir in:

500ml (16floz) *Vegetable Stock, 17*

Cook, covered, over medium heat to steam and heat through. To serve, mound the couscous in the centre of a large platter and surround it with the vegetables. Garnish with:

10 fresh mint leaves

Harissa

About 5 tablespoons

In North Africa, this fiery pepper paste is stirred into black olives, seafood stews, soups, herb salads and vegetable dishes, or used as an ingredient in sauces for brochettes, tagines and couscous. Combine in a small dry frying pan over medium heat and toast, shaking the pan often to prevent burning, until very aromatic, 2 to 3 minutes:

1 tsp caraway seeds

1 tsp coriander seeds

½ tsp cumin seeds

Remove from the heat, let cool to room temperature and grind to a fine powder in a spice grinder, coffee grinder or blender, or with a pestle and mortar. Add and grind again until smooth:

2 cloves garlic, quartered

Salt to taste

Add and grind until all the ingredients are well combined:

3 tbsp sweet paprika

1 tbsp crushed chilli flakes

1 tbsp olive oil

The harissa will be very thick and dry. Transfer the paste to a small jar and cover with:

Olive oil

Store, covered, in the refrigerator; it will keep for 6 months.

Ras El Hanout

About 125ml (4floz)

Morocco's ras el hanout contains many different elements, from seeds, leaves, flowers, roots and bark to Spanish fly beetle, a supposed aphrodisiac. Mix together thoroughly:

2 tbsp ground ginger

2 tsp ground black pepper

2 tsp ground allspice

2 tsp ground nutmeg

2 tsp ground mace

2 tsp ground cardamom

2 tsp ground cinnamon

2 tsp ground turmeric

1 tsp ground coriander

¼ tsp ground cloves

¼ tsp cayenne pepper

ABOUT
EGGS

The egg is nature's perfect shape. It is not surprising that so elegant a container should turn out to hold a small treasure of balanced nutrients – protein, fats, vitamins and minerals. The egg's unique properties give it a unique versatility. Eggs bind vegetables, tenderize timbales and provide richness to savoury puddings and custards. They also give lift to ethereal main-course soufflés.

Spinach Soufflé, 124

Composition and Nutrition

The egg's shell is made of hard but slightly porous calcium carbonate and lined on the inside and outside with protective membranes. Most eggs are washed before coming to market, which removes the outside membrane or cuticle; a light coating of mineral oil is often applied to replace it. The colour of the shell is an indication of the breed of the hen and has no connection with the quality of the egg or of its flavour. Brown shells are preferred by some cooks, and certain species of chickens lay yellow or even light pink, green or blue eggs.

A single egg white from a large egg weighs about 30g (1oz), provides about 17 calories, is almost 90 percent water and is otherwise made up mostly of protein, with only trace amounts of vitamins and minerals. The yolk of the same egg, although smaller in size (weighing about 15g/½ oz), is far denser and is richer in calories (about 60), nutrients and flavour. Besides providing fat, cholesterol, vitamins and minerals, the yolk offers a bit of protein and a measure of lecithin – the compound with the ability to make sauces, like mayonnaise, thick and smooth. A whole egg contains all of the essential amino acids, an essential fatty acid called linoleic acid, 6 grams of protein, 4.5g of fat (1.5g of which are saturated), 213mg of cholesterol, 1g of carbohydrate, 60mg of potassium, and 65mg of sodium, as well as 13 vitamins – almost all except C and niacin.

We have been eating far fewer eggs in the last twenty years, in large part because of concern over cholesterol, which is found in ample supply in egg yolks. (Egg whites contain no cholesterol.) Recent studies, however, suggest that eating eggs in moderation has little effect on the level of blood cholesterol, and most nutritionists agree that eggs have a place in a well-rounded, well-balanced diet. If cholesterol is a concern, see *Making Egg Substitutes, opposite.*

Quality, Safety and Storing

The quality of an egg is largely a matter of how old it is; the best eggs are the freshest. Age is not the only determining factor, however. The shell naturally protects an egg, and if it is cracked or damaged, the contents will deteriorate rapidly; eggs with cracked, damaged or dirty shells should not be used. Also important are the variables of temperature (eggs should be stored at less than 4°C/40°F), humidity (the ideal range is 70 to 80 percent), and handling (which means prompt and frequent gathering, along with washing and oiling of the shell by the producer). A week-old egg, properly stored, can be fresher than an egg left at room temperature for just one day. Check the date or freshness code required on a box from a British Egg Information Service approved packing station. Always buy eggs from a refrigerated case.

Fresh eggs, if refrigerated without interruption, should retain their quality for at least 1 month, although the whites will become noticeably thinner. Because they are repeatedly exposed to warm air, eggs stored in those handy slots in the refrigerator door will deteriorate more quickly than those kept in their carton, set on an inside shelf.

If you are unsure of the age of your eggs, just before using them, place them in a bowl of cold water. Those that float – a sign that the egg inside has shrunk through extended moisture loss – are not usable. You can also break an egg into a clean bowl and smell it. An old or stale egg will smell like damp grass or straw and will taint any delicate or pure egg dishes.

The bacteria *Salmonella enteritidis,* which can cause illness and even death, is occasionally found in raw eggs, even uncracked eggs. While the risk remains extremely low (even infected eggs may not cause problems if properly stored and cooked), we recommend handling eggs carefully, particularly when cooking for young children, the elderly, pregnant women or anyone with a compromised immune system.

HOW TO SEPARATE EGGS

Separating eggs can be done with an egg separator or by hand.

1 To use an egg separator, place the device on the rim of a cup or small bowl. Crack the egg carefully into the centre. The white will run through the slits around the sides into the container below, while the yolk will sit in the depression of the separator.

2 To separate by hand, have three bowls ready. Holding an egg in one hand, tap the egg on the edge of one of the bowls to make an even, crosswise break. Holding the egg over a bowl, pull the edges apart until the eggshell is broken into halves. Some of the egg white will immediately flow into the bowl.

3 Pour the remaining egg back and forth from one half-shell to the other, letting more of the white flow into the bowl each time until only the yolk remains in the shell. During this shifting process, you will be able to tell quickly if there is any discolouration or off odour, in which case you should discard the entire egg immediately. Should the yolk break during this process, you can try to remove any yolk particles from the white with the corner of a paper towel moistened with cold water. If this fails, the white may still be used for anything other than beaten egg whites; even the smallest speck of yolk can prevent egg whites from frothing. If the white is fresh and speckless, transfer it to the second bowl and the yolk to the third.

MAKING EGG SUBSTITUTES

Most egg-replacement products are 98 to 99 percent egg whites and thus lack the yolk-rich taste of whole eggs. Egg whites are also apt to dry out when cooked. You can make your own egg substitute by gently mixing together 12 egg whites, 1 tablespoon vegetable oil, and ¼ tsp salt. About 80ml (3floz) of this mixture is the equivalent volume of a whole egg. You can also substitute egg whites for up to half of the whole eggs in a recipe. Allow for 1½ egg whites (or a scant 3 tbsp) for every whole egg you omit.

EGG GRADES AND SIZES

Most eggs sold in the supermarkets are labelled grade A-C, and come in four sizes (very large, large, medium and small). Grade A eggs should be clean, undamaged and conform to rigid specifications in terms of the size of the air space and texture of the white and yolk. Only packing centres, which have been subject to special registrations by the British Egg Information Council, are authorised to pack Grade A eggs. Grade B eggs have less rigorous specifications, and Grade C eggs are those that do not fit the specifications for A or B. These grades have no bearing on size or freshness. The most common egg size sold today is medium, and our recipes, unless they state otherwise, use medium eggs.

Sometimes it is convenient or necessary to weigh or measure eggs out of the shell. Any time you need only part of an egg, beat the egg slightly to make it easier to measure. Use the following conversions:

1 large egg white = 30ml (1floz) = 2 tbsp

1 large egg yolk = 15ml (½ floz) = 1 tbsp

Asparagus Frittata

4 servings

A frittata is the Italian version of an omelette. It is more robust than the classic French omelette and a bit easier to handle. Instead of trying to flip the frittata, we recommend popping it under the grill to cook the top side. Served in wedges, frittatas are delicious hot, warm, or at room temperature.

Heat in a large frying pan over medium heat:

2 tbsp olive oil

Add and cook until lightly browned, about 10 minutes:

125-185g (4-6oz) lightly steamed asparagus tips and pieces

Season with:

¼ tsp salt

⅛ tsp ground black pepper

Transfer the asparagus to a strainer to drain off the excess oil. Let cool completely.

Preheat the grill.

Meanwhile, beat together until smooth:

5 eggs

½ tsp salt

Pinch of ground black pepper

Add the cooled asparagus along with:

45g (1½ oz) grated Parmesan cheese (optional)

1 tbsp chopped fresh parsley

Heat in a large, ovenproof frying pan over medium heat:

2 tbsp olive oil or 30g (1oz) butter

When hot, pour in the egg mixture.

Reduce the heat and cook until the bottom is set, then place under the grill for 30 to 60 seconds to finish cooking. A traditional frittata is not browned. Loosen the frittata with a flat metal spatula and slide it onto a plate. Cut into wedges.

ZUCCHINI FRITTATA

Prepare *Asparagus Frittata*, left, substituting 3 medium courgettes (zucchini), sliced, and 125g (4oz) thinly sliced onions for the asparagus. Add 1 tbsp finely shredded fresh basil with the Parmesan cheese and parsley.

Artichoke Frittata

8 servings

Cut off the stem and top two-thirds of:

6 medium artichokes

Place the artichokes bottom side up on the work surface and cut away the dark green outer leaves with quick, short strokes, beginning at the stem and working out. Once the white flesh is exposed, trim off all the remaining leaves. Scoop out the centre choke area with a grapefruit spoon or tsp and cut the artichoke bottom into 8 pieces.

Melt in a large, well-seasoned cast-iron frying pan over medium heat:

45g (1½oz) unsalted butter

Add and cook, stirring, until softened but not browned, about 5 minutes:

2 medium leeks, cleaned thoroughly and chopped

1 large clove garlic, chopped

Add the artichoke pieces along with:

180ml (6floz) water

1 tbsp fresh lemon juice

Cover and simmer over medium-low heat until the artichoke hearts are just tender, 12 to 15 minutes. Add more water if needed. Meanwhile roast, 58, peel, seed and thinly slice:

1 red pepper

Whisk together:

12 large eggs

310ml (½ pint) single cream

90g (3oz) grated Parmesan cheese

15g (½ oz) chopped fresh basil

1 tsp salt

Ground black pepper to taste

Preheat the grill.

When the artichokes are just tender, remove the lid and cook until the liquid is evaporated. Add:

30g (1oz) butter

Swirl to melt and coat the pan. Give the egg mixture a quick whisking and add to the pan. Stir in the roast peppers. Cook the frittata over medium-low heat until the centre is almost set, about 18 minutes. If desired, cook the frittata under the grill until browned, about 2 minutes. Cool to warm and serve from the pan in thin slices.

Huevos Rancheros

4 servings

In this classic Mexican dish, fried eggs are placed on a tortilla, then smothered with a spicy, rustic tomato chilli pepper sauce. Typically, these eggs are accompanied with Refried Beans, 81.

Prepare and keep warm:

500ml (16floz) Roast Tomato-Chipotle Salsa, right

In a large, nonstick frying pan, heat over medium-high heat:

1-2 tbsp vegetable oil

When hot, add 1 at a time and quick-fry for 2 to 3 seconds each side:

4 corn tortillas

Remove to paper towels to drain, then wrap in foil and keep warm in a very low oven. Place the frying pan over medium-low heat (or use two frying pans if the eggs will not all fit at once) and add a bit more oil if needed. Break into the pan:

4-8 eggs

Let cook until set. Cover the pan for a minute or so for the most even cooking. Season with:

Salt and ground black pepper to taste

Set a tortilla on each of 4 warmed plates and top with 1 or 2 eggs. Spoon a generous 125ml (4floz) of the warm tomato-chipotle sauce around each serving. Serve immediately sprinkled with:

Finely crumbled Mexican queso fresco, curd cheese or feta cheese

Chopped fresh coriander

Roast Tomato – Chipotle Salsa

About 500ml (16floz)

Tomatoes — and the salsa they create — take on a deeper flavour when roasted. Chipotle peppers (dried smoked jalapeños) have made great gains in popularity for their intense, rich, smoky flavour. They show up everywhere, from salsas and tinned tomato sauce (adobo) to stews, soups and more.

Build a medium-low fire in your barbecue or preheat the grill. Place on the barbecue or grill pan:

6 medium, ripe tomatoes, seeded, if desired, and halved

Barbecue or grill as close to the heat as possible, turning as needed, until the skins are blackened in spots and slightly softened, about 5 minutes each side on the barbecue and slightly less time in the grill. When cool enough to handle, remove the skins and coarsely chop the tomatoes, put them in a medium bowl and stir in:

1 small onion, finely chopped, rinsed, and drained

4 tbsp coarsely chopped fresh coriander

3 tbsp fresh lime juice, or to taste

2 tbsp olive oil

2 cloves garlic, finely chopped

1½ tsp finely chopped tinned chipotle pepper, or to taste

1 tsp ground cumin

Salt to taste

Serve immediately.

Vegetable Timbale

4 servings

Timbale is the French word for "kettle drum" and refers to any savoury custard baked in a small, high-sided, drum-shaped mould. In its modern usage, a timbale is any savoury custard cooked in an individual mould and then inverted and unmoulded before serving.

Position a rack in the lower third of the oven. Preheat the oven to 165°C (325°F) Gas 3. Lightly grease four 185g (6oz) ramekins.

Steam or blanch until crisp-tender:

250g (8oz) coarsely chopped cauliflower florets, broccoli florets or courgettes or 375g (12oz) sweetcorn kernels

Drain thoroughly and either finely chop or pulse in a food processor.

Transfer to a bowl. Melt in a small frying pan over medium heat:

15g (½oz) unsalted butter

Add and cook, stirring, until softened, 2 to 3 minutes:

4 tbsp chopped shallots (about 2)

Add to the vegetables and season with:

2 tbsp Madeira (optional)

½ tsp salt

⅛ tsp freshly grated or ground nutmeg

Ground black pepper to taste

Heat almost to a boil:

250ml (8floz) single or double cream

Whisk into the vegetables:

3 large eggs

Slowly whisk in the hot cream and ladle the custard into the prepared dishes. Sprinkle the tops with:

4 tbsp grated Parmesan cheese

Place the dishes in a water bath (opposite). Cover the tin with foil and bake until the custard is set two-thirds of the way to the centre of the dishes, 25 to 30 minutes. Remove from the oven, loosen the cover but leave it on and return to the oven to cook for another 10 minutes. Let cool for 10 minutes, then run a knife around the inside edge of the ramekins. Invert the timbales onto serving plates. Serve sprinkled with:

Chopped fresh parsley or snipped fresh chives (optional)

Sweetcorn Pudding with Roast Poblano Peppers

6 servings

Position a rack in the centre of the oven. Butter a 1.5 litre (2½ pint) gratin or soufflé dish.
Roast, 58:

3 poblano or New Mexico green chilli peppers

Peel, remove the seeds and veins, then chop.
Cut and scrape the kernels from:

4 ears sweetcorn

Heat in a large frying pan over medium heat:

30g (1oz) butter or 2 tbsp corn oil

Add and cook for 5 minutes:

1 onion, diced
2 tsp finely chopped garlic

½ tsp dried oregano

Stir in the sweetcorn kernels and roast peppers. Cook for 3 minutes, then let cool. Combine in another bowl:

4 large eggs, lightly beaten
90g (3oz) grated mild Cheddar or Muenster cheese
60g (2oz) grated mature Cheddar cheese
Salt and ground black pepper to taste

Add the cooled sweetcorn mixture and scrape into the prepared dish. Bake until puffed and golden, about 30 minutes.

Spoon Bread

6 to 8 servings

This corn bread is soft enough to eat with a spoon or fork. For a light meal, sprinkle with grated cheese or add a dollop of sour cream and spicy salsa on the side and serve with a green salad.

Position a rack in the centre of the oven. Preheat the oven to 190°C (375°F) Gas 5. Grease a 20 x 20cm (8 x 8in) baking dish.
In a large, heavy saucepan, bring to a simmer:

625ml (1 pint) milk
30g (1oz) unsalted butter
1 tsp salt

Reduce the heat to low. Add in a slow, steady stream, whisking constantly to prevent lumps:

125g (4oz) cornmeal

Increase the heat to medium and cook, stirring constantly, until the mixture is thick and shiny,
3 to 4 minutes. Remove from the heat and set aside to cool for 3 to 4 minutes. Whisk together:

3 large egg yolks
125ml (4floz) cream or milk

Stir gradually into the cornmeal mixture. Beat on medium speed until the peaks are stiff but not dry:

3 large egg whites
⅛ tsp cream of tartar (optional)

Fold one-quarter of the egg whites into the cornmeal mixture to lighten it, then fold in the remaining whites. Scrape the batter into the baking dish and spread evenly. Bake until the bread has risen like a soufflé, with a golden brown surface, and a knife inserted in the centre comes out clean, 25 to 35 minutes. Serve immediately.

THE WATER BATH

By baking a dish of custard in a larger pan of water, also known as the bain-marie or "Maria's bath", the cook partially insulates the custard from the oven's heat and thereby protects it from over-cooking. All you need is a roasting tin large enough to accommodate the custards comfortably. Set a cake rack in the tin or cover the pan bottom with a tea towel or several layers of paper towels so the custards will not be in direct contact with the hot tin bottom. Arrange the custards in the dry tin, slip the pan into a preheated oven, and immediately pour enough scalding-hot tap water into the tin to come one-half to two-thirds of the way up the sides of the custard dishes.

Tomato and Goat's Cheese Quiche

One 23cm (9in) quiche; 6 servings

The most famous of savoury custards is quiche, a custard containing small bits of vegetables and/or cheese baked in a pastry crust. The basic proportions are 3 to 4 whole eggs for every 500ml (16floz) of milk. Using cream in place of milk or replacing one whole egg with 2 yolks gives you a richer, more custardy quiche. Quiche is traditionally prepared in a prebaked pastry case brushed with egg yolk to help prevent it from becoming soggy. Tomato and goat's cheese make an excellent quiche, but fillings are endlessly variable.

Prepare:

½ recipe Flaky Pastry, below

Roll out the pastry 2mm (⅛ in) thick and fit into a buttered 23cm (9in) quiche or flan dish. Refrigerate while you prepare the filling. Set a rack in the lowest position in the oven. Preheat the oven to 200°C (400°F) Gas 6.

Prepare and set aside:

500g (1lb) plum tomatoes (about 6), cored, quartered lengthwise and seeded

Crumble into a bowl:

125g (4oz) fresh goat's cheese

Slowly mash in with the back of a wooden spoon until smooth:

180ml (6floz) single or double cream

125ml (4floz) milk

Add and whisk until smooth:

3 large eggs

1 tbsp chopped fresh parsley

1½ tsp chopped fresh thyme or savoury or 3 tbsp chopped fresh basil

¼ tsp salt

Plenty of ground black pepper

Remove the pastry case from the refrigerator and arrange the tomato quarters in the shell like the spokes of a wheel, with the pointed end towards the centre of the quiche. Fill in the centre with more tomato quarters. Pour the cheese mixture over the tomatoes and bake until the pastry and top are golden brown, 40 to 45 minutes. Let the quiche rest for 10 minutes to settle, then cut into wedges and serve.

Flaky Pastry

Two 23cm (9in) pastry shells, or one 23cm (9in) double crust pie

This dough makes a light, flaky crust that shatters at the touch of a fork. If you need only a single pastry shell, decrease all ingredients by half or freeze half the dough for future use.

Using a rubber spatula, thoroughly mix in a large bowl:

375g (12oz) plain flour

1 tsp white sugar or 1 tbsp icing sugar

1 tsp salt

Add:

250g (8oz) vegetable lard, or 125g (4oz) lard and 125g (4oz) cold unsalted butter

Break the lard into large chunks; if using butter, cut it into small pieces, then add it to the flour mixture. Cut the fat into the dry ingredients by chopping vigorously with a pastry blender or by cutting in opposite directions with 2 knives, one held in each hand. As you work, periodically stir dry flour up from the bottom of the bowl and scrape clinging fat off the pastry blender or knives. When you have finished, some of the fat should remain in pea-sized pieces; the rest should be reduced to the consistency of coarse crumbs or cornmeal. The mixture should seem dry and powdery and not pasty or greasy. Drizzle over the flour and fat mixture:

6 tbsp iced water

Using the rubber spatula, cut with the blade side until the mixture looks evenly moistened and begins to form small balls. Press down on the dough with the flat side of the spatula. If the balls of dough stick together, you have added enough water; if they do not, drizzle over the top:

1-2 tbsp iced water

Cut in the water, again using the blade of the spatula, then press with your hands until the dough coheres. The pastry should look rough, not smooth. Divide the pastry in half, press each half into a round flat disc, and wrap tightly in cling film. Refrigerate for at least 30 minutes, and preferably for several hours, or for up to 2 days before rolling. The pastry can also be wrapped airtight and frozen for up to 6 months; thaw completely before rolling.

Spinach Soufflé

6 servings

Preheat the oven to 190°C (375°F) Gas 5. Generously butter a 1 litre (1½ pint) soufflé dish or six 250ml (8floz) ramekins and dust the insides with:

30-45g (1-1½oz) dried breadcrumbs or grated Parmesan cheese

Shake out the excess. Combine in a bowl or large saucepan:

375ml (12floz) *Thick Béchamel Sauce, opposite,* at room temperature or slightly warmed

¾ tsp salt

⅛ tsp ground nutmeg or red pepper

Pinch of ground white pepper

Beat 125ml (4floz) of the mixture into:

6 large egg yolks

75g (2½oz) grated Parmesan or Swiss cheese, or a combination

Combine with the rest of the sauce, beating vigorously to blend. Add:

500g (1lb) cooked spinach, squeezed dry and finely chopped

Beat until stiff but not dry:

6 large egg whites

Pinch of salt

Stir one-quarter of the whites into the soufflé base to lighten it, then fold in the rest. Pour into the prepared soufflé dish or ramekins. Bake until the soufflé is risen and golden brown on top, 40 to 45 minutes (20 to 25 minutes for individual soufflés). Remove from the oven and serve immediately.

CARROT SOUFFLÉ

Prepare *Spinach Soufflé, left,* substituting puréed cooked carrots for the spinach. Add 1 tbsp chopped fresh thyme or dill to the base.

MUSHROOM SOUFFLÉ

Prepare *Spinach Soufflé, left,* substituting sautéed finely chopped mushrooms (preferably chestnut) for the spinach. If desired, 45-90g (1½-3oz) grated Gruyère cheese can be substituted for the Parmesan. For additional herbs, try 1½ tsp chopped fresh marjoram or rosemary.

Make-Ahead Goat's Cheese and Walnut Soufflés

8 servings

These are more substantial than traditional soufflés, but they are wonderful in their own right. Serve them on a lightly dressed bed of field greens.

Preheat the oven to 180°C (350°F) Gas 4.

Combine:

90g (3oz) walnuts, toasted and finely chopped

30g (1oz) cornmeal

Generously butter eight 180ml (6floz) ramekins and sprinkle the insides with the cornmeal mixture, tilting in all directions until completely coated. Scatter any nuts that do not adhere over the bottoms of the dishes. Melt in a saucepan over medium heat:

45g (1½ oz) unsalted butter

Stir in until smooth:

4 tbsp plain flour

Cook, stirring, for 1 minute. Remove from the heat and stir in:

160ml (5floz) milk

Return to the heat and, stirring very briskly, bring to a boil. (The mixture will be very thick.) Scrape into a bowl. Add and mash until the cheese is melted:

315g (10oz) fresh goat's cheese

Beat in:

4 large egg yolks

2 cloves garlic, very finely chopped

¼ tsp dried thyme

¼ tsp salt

¼ tsp ground white pepper

Beat until stiff but not dry:

5 large egg whites

¼ tsp cream of tartar

Stir one-quarter of the whites into the soufflé base to lighten it, then fold in the rest. Pour into the prepared ramekins and smooth the tops. Place the ramekins in a water bath, 121. Bake until a skewer inserted in the centre comes out almost clean, about 30 minutes. Let stand for 15 minutes in the water bath, then invert the ramekins onto a greased baking tray. The soufflés can be served immediately or cooled, covered tightly with cling film, and refrigerated for up to 3 days. When ready to serve, heat the soufflés in a 220°C (425°F) Gas 7 oven until warmed through, 5 to 7 minutes.

Sauce Béchamel (White Sauce)

About 250ml (8floz)

Combine in a small saucepan over very low heat:

300ml (½ pint) milk

¼ onion with 1 bay leaf stuck to it using 2 whole cloves

Pinch of freshly grated nutmeg (optional)

Simmer gently for 15 minutes, uncovered, to infuse flavour into the milk. Discard the onion, bay leaf and cloves. Meanwhile, melt in a medium, heavy saucepan over low heat:

30g (1oz) unsalted butter

Stir in:

2 tbsp plain flour

Cook, uncovered, stirring occasionally with a wooden spoon or spatula, over medium-low heat until the roux is just fragrant but not darkened, 2 to 3 minutes. Remove from the heat and let cool slightly. Slowly whisk in the warm milk and return the saucepan to the heat. Bring the sauce slowly to a simmer, whisking to prevent lumps. Cook, stirring often and skimming any skin that forms on the surface, over low heat, without boiling, until it reaches the consistency of thick cream soup, 8 to 10 minutes. Strain through a fine-mesh sieve, if desired. Season with:

Salt and ground white pepper to taste

THIN BÉCHAMEL SAUCE

Use as a quick base for cream soups.
Prepare *Sauce Béchamel, above,* decreasing the butter to 15g (½ oz) and the flour to 1 tablespoon. The finished sauce should be thick enough to coat the back of a spoon.

THICK BÉCHAMEL SAUCE

Use as a soufflé base or to bind a runny casserole.
Prepare *Sauce Béchamel, above,* increasing the butter to 45g (1½ oz) and the flour to 3 tablespoons.

RULES FOR SOUFFLÉS

● Soufflés are best baked in straight-sided moulds – so they can rise up tall – that are generously buttered with soft, not melted, butter and dusted with grated cheese or breadcrumbs.

● The savoury soufflé base of *Thick Béchamel Sauce, left,* can be made up to 2 days in advance and stored in the refrigerator. Warm it to lukewarm about 1 hour before you plan to serve the soufflés.

● Adding 1 or 2 additional egg whites for every 4 whole eggs used will produce a soufflé with more height and a lighter texture.

● The egg whites must be folded into the base as soon as they are whipped to stiff, but not dry, peaks.

● Soufflé moulds should be filled to within 2.5-1cm (1-½in) of the rim – if higher, the soufflé may spill over the sides during baking.

● Before baking, run your thumb around the inside rim of the mould, making a 2.5cm (1in) groove in the soufflé mixture; for individual moulds, make a 1cm (½in) groove. This will promote an even rise and give the cooked soufflé a top-hat appearance.

● Bake the soufflés on a baking tray for ease of moving them in and out of the oven, and place the tray on the bottom rack of the oven to make room for the soufflés' anticipated rise.

Index

ACKNOWLEDGEMENTS

Special thanks to my wife and editor in residence, Susan; our indispensable assistant and comrade, Mary Gilbert; and our friends and agents, Gene Winick and Sam Pinkus. Much appreciation also goes to Simon & Schuster, Scribner, and Weldon Owen for their devotion to this project. Thank you Carolyn, Susan, Bill, Marah, John, Terry, Roger, Gaye, Val, Norman and all the other capable and talented folks who gave a part of themselves to the Joy of Cooking All About series.

My eternal appreciation goes to the food experts, writers and editors whose contributions and collaborations are at the heart of Joy — especially Stephen Schmidt. He was to the 1997 edition what Chef Pierre Adrian was to Mom's final editions of Joy. Thank you one and all.

Ethan Becker

FOOD EXPERTS, WRITERS, AND EDITORS

Selma Abrams, Jody Adams, Samia Ahad, Bruce Aidells, Katherine Alford, Deirdre Allen, Pam Anderson, Elizabeth Andoh, Phillip Andres, Alice Arndt, John Ash, Nancy Baggett, Rick and Deann Bayless, Lee E. Benning, Rose Levy Beranbaum, Brigit Legere Binns, Jack Bishop, Carole Bloom, Arthur Boehm, Ed Brown, JeanMarie Brownson, Larry Catanzaro, Val Cipollone, Polly Clingerman, Elaine Corn, Bruce Cost, Amy Cotler, Brian Crawley, Gail Damerow, Linda Dann, Deirdre Davis, Jane Spencer Davis, Erica De Mane, Susan Derecskey, Abigail Johnson Dodge, Jim Dodge, Aurora Esther, Michele Fagerroos, Eva Forson, Margaret Fox, Betty Fussell, Mary Gilbert, Darra Goldstein, Elaine Gonzalez, Dorie Greenspan, Maria Guarnaschelli, Helen Gustafson, Pat Haley, Gordon Hamersley, Melissa Hamilton, Jessica Harris, Hallie Harron, Nao Hauser, William Hay, Larry Hayden, Kate Hays, Marcella Hazan, Tim Healea, Janie Hibler, Lee Hofstetter, Paula Hogan, Rosemary Howe, Mike Hughes, Jennifer Humphries, Dana Jacobi, Stephen Johnson, Lynne Rossetto Kasper, Denis Kelly, Fran Kennedy, Johanne Killeen and George Germon, Shirley King, Maya Klein, Diane M. Kochilas, Phyllis Kohn, Aglaia Kremezi, Mildred Kroll, Loni Kuhn, Corby Kummer, Virginia Lawrence, Jill Leigh, Karen Levin, Lori Longbotham, Susan Hermann Loomis, Emily Luchetti, Stephanie Lyness, Karen MacNeil, Deborah Madison, Linda Marino, Kathleen McAndrews, Alice Medrich, Anne Mendelson, Lisa Montenegro, Cindy Mushet, Marion Nestle, Toby Oksman, Joyce O'Neill, Suzen O'Rourke, Russ Parsons, Holly Pearson, James Peterson, Marina Petrakos, Mary Placek, Maricel Presilla, Marion K. Pruitt, Adam Rapoport, Mardee Haidin Regan, Peter Reinhart, Sarah Anne Reynolds, Madge Rosenberg, Nicole Routhier, Jon Rowley, Nancy Ross Ryan, Chris Schlesinger, Stephen Schmidt, Lisa Schumacher, Marie Simmons, Nina Simonds, A. Cort Sinnes, Sue Spitler, Marah Stets, Molly Stevens, Christopher Stoye, Susan Stuck, Sylvia Thompson, Jean and Pierre Troisgros, Jill Van Cleave, Patricia Wells, Laurie Wenk, Caroline Wheaton, Jasper White, Jonathan White, Marilyn Wilkenson, Carla Williams, Virginia Willis, John Willoughby, Deborah Winson, Lisa Yockelson.

Weldon Owen wishes to thank the following people and organizations for their generous assistance and support in producing this book: Desne Border, Ken DellaPenta, Oldways Preservation & Exchange Trust and Joan Olson.